# AMERICAN HEROES COMING OUT FROM BEHIND THE BADGE

*Stories from Police, Fire, and EMS Professionals "Out" on the Job*

## GREG MIRAGLIA

authorHOUSE®

*AuthorHouse™*
*1663 Liberty Drive*
*Bloomington, IN 47403*
*www.authorhouse.com*
*Phone: 1-800-839-8640*

*First published by AuthorHouse  12/29/2010*

*ISBN: 978-1-4520-7627-0 (sc)*
*ISBN: 978-1-4520-7628-7 (dj)*
*ISBN: 978-1-4520-7629-4 (e)*

*Library of Congress Control Number: 2010917075*

*Printed in the United States of America*

*This book is printed on acid-free paper.*

*Certain stock imagery © Thinkstock.*

There are so many good friends and family who have helped me to become who I am today. Their unconditional love allowed me to develop my passions, to achieve my goals, and to eventually share my truth with the world. I am lucky to have so many people in my life who support and encourage me every day.

This book is dedicated to my husband, partner, and best friend Tony. Your love fills and inspires me every day. It is also dedicated to my parents, Arlene and Ray, who have supported and encouraged me every day of my life. When I came out, they loved me even more. They showed me the true power of living a life in the truth through their unconditional love. I could not ask for more nurturing parents who gave me everything I needed to be successful in this life. Thank you.

# CONTENTS

# INTRODUCTION

In 1978, being gay and out in law enforcement was unheard of except in larger police departments like San Francisco's. In fact, it was just a few years before that the American Psychological Association removed homosexuality from its list of mental illnesses. There was no employment protection based on sexual orientation, and police departments were still asking about homosexual experiences as part of the standard background investigation conducted for every law enforcement applicant. While it had been nine years since the Stonewall Riots, in California, the gay rights movement was really just coming alive. Harvey Milk was elected to the San Francisco Board of Supervisors as the first openly gay public official in the country. The Castro neighborhood in San Francisco was emerging as the focal point on the West Coast for the gay rights movement.

I started my career at a medium-sized police department at the age of fourteen as a police explorer scout. Within the first hour of being in the police department, I knew that I could not be "out" and have a successful law enforcement career. I knew that I was gay, but I made a decision to hide in order to pursue a law enforcement career. I spent the next twenty-five years leading two separate lives. I literally hid behind my badge, thinking somehow that no one would ever suspect a guy who was good at playing the part of a straight man and who was enjoying a very successful career. I never dated women, but I always showed up with an attractive woman on my arm at the department social events. On my days off, I would hook up with guys for one-night stands but would never disclose my real identity or profession. I buried myself in my work to avoid the inevitable loneliness that comes with being in the closet.

Finally, in 2004, I mustered the courage to come out from behind my badge and to begin living my life in the truth. In 2006, I married the love of my life, Tony. I'm still enjoying a very successful career administering and teaching at a law enforcement academy at Napa Valley College in California. As I looked back, I realized that I had remained in the closet out of fear for way too long. The pain, fear, and loneliness I experienced were for naught. While I'm confident that I would not be where I am today had I come out in 1978, I can say with some certainty that times have changed. There are many highly successful gay police officers, male and female, working across the country at all levels of large and small police and sheriff departments. There are also way too many gay and lesbian police officers who remain hidden in the closet.

I wrote the first book, *Coming Out from Behind the Badge*, because when I came out, there were no books about being gay and out in law enforcement. The only ones I found were about ten years old and contained many stories of devastation and career-ending failure after coming out. I knew that my experience in 2004 was different from those told in the books published in 1994. Society had changed, and I knew that there had to be other success stories out there that needed to be told. My partner, Tony, was the person who really inspired me to write. He encouraged me to share my truth and my experience with the hope of inspiring others to come out from behind the badge. The first book was published in late 2007, and from the day it was released, I began searching for more stories to share for this book.

I'm often asked about how I collected the stories and who wrote them. I solicited contributions on a website that I created while researching the first book. I sent out invitations to every LGBT law enforcement organization I could find. All of the stories I received were written by the contributors based on the idea of the book I pitched on the website. While the stories were different, they all came from people who sincerely wanted to make a difference in the lives of other LGBT officers. Like the first edition, this book contains stories written by the officers themselves from around the country. In addition to more stories from law enforcement officers, I've included contributions from a firefighter and a transgender EMS professional.

I tried not to edit out the "voice" of the author, as I believe this is how best to really hear the individual stories. Some of the stories are lengthier than others. In fact, the story of San Francisco Police Sergeant Peter Thoshinsky occupies almost half of this book. His words are thoughtful, and his passion for the job and what he has to share are more than worthy of these pages. In the second section, I share my thoughts today about coming out. The intent of this edition—like the first—is to inspire those who are still in the closet to come out. In this part of the book, I share my understanding of the coming-out process and suggest some ideas for how to move away from feelings of shame to those of pride. Finally, the last part of the book has website links and contact information for all of the LGBT public safety organizations we know about. They are here for your benefit with an open invitation to reach out for support and as evidence that you are not alone.

It is my hope that these stories will also be read by our straight allies and those who have yet to understand what it is like to be gay in law enforcement. Clearly there is no way to fully understand how much courage it takes to come out in law enforcement unless you have faced having to do it, but I hope these stories give some sense of what these individuals experienced. I hope at least that they will help you understand and to better empathize with someone you work with who may be hiding behind his or her badge. It makes little difference whether you work in law enforcement, the fire service, or as an EMS professional; we all depend on one another. Your gay and lesbian colleagues want the same thing you do. We all want the benefits of camaraderie and the great feeling that comes from being able to depend on someone as well as to be depended upon. We want to know those we work with and to know their truths. Being closeted compromises all of this. In the worst of cases, it has caused officers to take their own lives.

If this book inspires just one police officer, deputy sheriff, firefighter, or EMS professional to come out, I will feel completely satisfied. If these stories give just one straight person a better understanding of their co-workers, I've accomplished what I set out to do. If just one chief or one sheriff works to change his or her agency's culture to be welcoming and accepting of the LGBT employees who likely already work there, mission accomplished. Enjoy the stories.

# Out On the Job and Proud of It—Greg Miraglia

As I sat in the courtroom in the Phillip Burton Federal Building in San Francisco, I remembered my last visit some fifteen years earlier while testifying as an expert witness for a workplace discrimination and sexual harassment lawsuit. The shiny marble, tall ceilings, and mahogany furniture make you feel cold, reserved, and just a bit intimidated. The large seal of the United States federal district court hung on the wall above the judge's seat, and a lone American flag sat to the right of the bench. The gallery benches were much like the pews I remembered from church, designed purposely to be uncomfortable so that one couldn't dose off if one tried. As I looked around the room and listened to the quiet whispers, the room did in fact feel much like a church. There is a certain similar reverence in a courtroom as there is in a church, and I'm sure a great deal of praying goes on in both venues during the normal course of the business. But today, I wasn't there for a trial or to testify. It was for something even more surreal.

The day's event began with a DEA agent taking his place at the podium and welcoming the 150 or so people in the room to the very first multiagency pride celebration for the Federal Bureau of Investigation,

Drug Enforcement Administration, United States Attorney's Office, and General Services Administration. It was June 30, 2010, the last day of National Pride Month and the very first pride celebration event for the LGBT employees of these federal agencies. There we were sitting in a federal courtroom on the same floor of the federal building where Judge Walker heard the first federal same-sex marriage case.

The FBI's special agent in charge of the five-hundred-person San Francisco office was the first to speak. She introduced all of her second-in-commands who were also in the room and who all were there to support their LGBT colleagues. As I listened to her speak and stared at the United States seal on the big marble wall, I started to realize how much has changed in my lifetime relative to the gay community. In the year I was born, 1963, this same group would have assembled in this federal courtroom not to celebrate gay pride, but to hear a criminal trial with the FBI on one side of the investigation and the gays on the other. There would not have been a celebration taking place and certainly no feelings of pride. And certainly, if there were any gay members of the FBI in the room, they would have either been deeply closeted or sitting at the defendant's table fighting for their jobs or defending themselves against a criminal charge related to being gay, because in that year, sodomy and many other homosexual acts were illegal.

I was invited to this event to be the keynote speaker representing the Matthew Shepard Foundation and my colleagues on the board of directors. My husband, Tony, sat next to me as I listened to my introduction. Here are some of the words I shared with the audience that day.

> Thank you for the great honor of representing the Matthew Shepard Foundation, and on behalf of my good friends Judy and Dennis Shepard, their son Logan, and my colleagues on the Board of Directors of the Matthew Shepard Foundation, congratulations for coming together to celebrate Pride Month.
>
> I'd like you to stop for just a minute and think about where we all are today. Here we sit in a federal courtroom celebrating gay pride. Remember, the whole idea of a

pride celebration started with a violence confrontation between the police and the gay community. And today, we have come together, out and proud members of law enforcement, to celebrate gay pride in a federal courtroom.

Let me begin by telling you briefly about the Matthew Shepard Foundation and what it is we do. Our primary mission includes replacing hate with understanding, compassion, and acceptance. Since Matt was murdered twelve years ago, our most major effort was to get federal hate crimes law changed to include sexual orientation and gender identity. As everyone in this room knows, we finally got it done in October 2009 with the Matthew Shepard and James Byrd, Jr. Hate Crimes Protection Act. And even though California has been way ahead in this area, this new act will provide much needed support for local law enforcement's efforts to investigate and prosecute hate crimes by providing invaluable support from many of the agencies represented in this room.

I never knew Matthew Shepard—or *Matt* Shepard, as he was known to his close friends and family. From talking with his parents and close friends, I know that just before his murder, Matt discovered a passion for political science and dreamed of someday changing the world. Matt never understood how one person could hate another simply because of who they were. After seeing what has happened after this death, I believe Matt has changed the world in ways he could have never imagined. His story has created many visible changes, but many more that are largely invisible, and I would like to share just one of them with you today.

In 1978, I was a freshman in high school and started my law enforcement career as a police explorer scout. I knew I was gay, and I discovered quickly that I could not be out and successful in law enforcement at the same time. At the time Matt was murdered, I remember hearing about it but didn't pay close attention to the details about what happened. In fact, it wasn't until 2001 after seeing a documentary called *Anatomy of a Hate Crime* that I learned the graphic details of this horrific hate crime. I was so moved by Matt's story that I wanted to do something about it, and this lead me to meeting Judy Shepard and getting involved with the foundation's educational work.

In the years that followed, I shared Matt's story with various groups, including my students in the police academy where I was then working as the director. I traveled with Judy from time to time and heard her talk over and over again about the importance of coming out and sharing your story. She told audiences that this was the most effective way of changing hearts and minds and eliminating homophobia.

I felt good about my work with the foundation but knew I could do more. Finally in 2004, after hearing Judy's voice and thinking about Matt's story, I found the courage to come out. It was the most difficult thing I've ever done, and if it weren't for Matthew Shepard and my friendship with his mother, Judy, I don't know if I would have ever found the courage to do it. Of course, today, it's hard to remember what life was like before coming out, and I am but one of many people who Matt's life has changed forever.

Now despite all of my fears, what I have learned since coming out six years ago is that I severely underestimated my family and friends. I still believe that, as a profession, law enforcement is twenty years behind the rest of the civil rights movement in its acceptance and understanding of LGBT people, but I also never realized how right Judy

Shepard was about the power of sharing your story. Some of my colleagues in law enforcement were very homophobic. I can tell you with absolute certainty that, after I came out to them, their views about gay people changed for the better.

Sure, we can enact antidiscrimination and workplace harassment laws, but nothing is more powerful in changing the hearts and minds of our straight colleagues than to come out and to share your personal story. This is how we will eliminate homophobia in law enforcement. It is also how I believe we will truly achieve "liberty and justice for all." It takes courage and confidence to be out, much like it takes to be a justice employee. We all entered this vocation because we believe in principles of a free society and in service to others. But we cannot force people to change their attitudes and opinions with laws. We must use our personal stories to cause a free will change of heart. My partner, Tony, who is here with me today, has always told me that people will be as comfortable with you as you are with yourself.

To all of you who are out and proud here today, congratulations and thank you for your personal courage. Continue to have pride in the work you do and in who you are. You don't need to wait for June each year to celebrate your pride. Celebrate it daily.

I have to say that the entire event was first class. From the time Agent Kari called me the night before to introduce herself as our personal host and guide for the day to the presentation of a plaque to Tony and me in appreciation for participating, the FBI, DEA, GSA, and US Attorney's Office did it right. It was a very humbling experience to speak before such an amazing group of professionals, and I felt so proud to be among them as an out member of the law enforcement profession.

It seems like a lifetime ago that I started writing my first book, *Coming Out from Behind the Badge*, back in 2005. And yet, it was only five years ago that I started to write my story, but so much has happened since that time to me personally and in the world. No one gets rich from writing a book, and since I self-published the first book, I'm not sure that I've even broken even financially. It is used as a required textbook in an administration of justice class at Santa Rosa Junior College. However, the people I have met and the opportunities I've been given because of the book are all very special moments in my life and have made it all so worth it. The e-mails I've received from people—young and old—some out and many still deeply closeted, have brought both smiles and tears. My original goals for the book were pretty basic and included wanting to provide information and inspiration for LGBT law enforcement professionals to come out and to start living their lives as they were created to be. I've had the great honor of watching this actually happen, and it fills my heart with more joy than any amount I might have received from a royalty check.

So let me take you back and catch you up on what has happened since I wrote my story for the first book with the hope that you will see not only how coming out has changed my life entirely, but how society and the law enforcement profession is changing rapidly and for the better. When I think about my life before coming out, I cannot really remember how it felt, and I don't really remember who or how I was before I said those words on March 10, 2004, for the first time to another person. That day was like being reborn and becoming whole. Many of the days and months that followed were not without fear, intimidation, and some very uncomfortable moments, but it was so entirely worth it. My only regret is that I waited so long to do it.

Tony has told me on more than on occasion that I wouldn't be who I am today if I had come out earlier, and he reminds me that our path in life is full of reason and purpose. I'm pretty much over looking back and, while I would be lying if I said I didn't wish I was out when I was in my twenties, I know there is no way to go back now. Spending time regretting isn't productive and won't accomplish anything. Instead, I'm living life as a whole person every day and spending my time ridding myself of whatever residual guilt might still reside in my mind. I would be lying if I said it was easy, because it isn't. But if I have any regrets about any part of the process, actually coming out isn't one of them.

On January 27, 2008, I officially released the first book *Coming Out from Behind the Badge* and a website for the book. We held the release event at the A Different Light Bookstore, located in the heart of the Castro in San Francisco. I chose that place rather than a local bookstore because I had learned that already gay bookstores were suffering from the advent of e-books and the mainstreaming of gay literature. I spent so many years avoiding the Castro for fear of being seen that I wanted to "officially" come out with the book in the heart of the bay area's gay community. The Castro was also the place where the police and the gay community clashed and fought for many years. It is also the place that the great Harvey Milk lived, worked, and helped to mend the relationship between the police and the gay community. For me, the Castro was the only place to release a book about gay police.

As confident as I was about writing the book and as much of a desire as I had to want to help other gay cops, I was somewhat terrified as the release party began. For the better part of twenty-five years, I worked so hard to keep my private life a secret from everyone. And now, not only was I standing in the heart of the gay community I had avoided, but I was presenting all of my secrets to the world in print. Even though I had been out by then for almost four years, as Tony started the reading in front of a small crowd that gathered in the bookstore, my heart pounded. As expected, I signed a stack of books, received amazing support from friends and some strangers who attended the release event, and in just two hours, it was over, and the book was officially out.

In 2008, I was asked to facilitate a discussion about coming out at work and to sit on a panel of authors at the twelfth annual conference for LGBT law enforcement professionals in Washington DC. The conference was hosted by the DC-area Gay Officers Action League. If you are not aware, there are Law Enforcement Gay Action Leagues (LEGAL) and Gay Officer Action Leagues (GOAL) that are both part of an international organization. There are many LEGAL and GOAL groups located around the country in some places where you might least expect them to be, including Alabama and Iowa. We have a list of all of these gay law enforcement organizations listed on the book website at www.comingoutfrombehindthebadge.com and in the appendix of this book.

Anyway, the conference that year was scheduled during the same week as National Police Week in Washington DC. This is an annual event held each year to honor those officers who died in the line of duty the previous year. It's a major event for the law enforcement profession. There is a huge memorial there that includes the names of every peace officer killed in the line of duty. Family members and colleagues travel to this memorial to remember their loved one and to copy the etching of his or her name from the granite slabs that create the memorial space.

It just so happened that Aaron, one of the program coordinators at the police academy who worked for me, had been trying to get me to go to police week with him and a group of officers who attend annually. Since the conference was the same week, I decided to go this year. I was to room with Aaron and one of the other officers who was coordinating this trip. I told Aaron about the conference, and he immediately expressed total support and an interest in coming to the session I was to facilitate. I was excited about the trip, as I had not been to DC before, but I felt uneasy about traveling with a group of straight guys who, other than Aaron, I was not yet out to. Before coming out, I found so much more in common with my straight colleagues because there was nothing exposed about me that was uncommon. I could "hang" with the guys in a bar, drink, talk shop, and fit right in. But things were now different, and for the first time, I really experienced discomfort and a lack of commonality with these colleagues.

The first night we were in DC, the group went out for dinner to what I was told would be a place with "really great food." Apparently, even my taste buds had changed, because the food was horrible. Everyone else at the table was raving about it. I didn't know most of the people who were at the table with me. Many were from a sheriff's department a couple of counties away. There were men and women around the table all talking about what shift they were working, department politics—the usual stuff cops talk about. The women were talking like sailors and swore more than I did on a bad day. It was interesting to watch them try to fit in with their male co-workers. One couple was there secretly away from their respective spouses. Apparently, they had been having an affair for some time and saw this trip as a way to spend time together. As I sat listening to the banter and watching the posturing going on, I really felt completely out of place and never more different. For so long, I felt entirely comfortable in a social gathering of cops, but something felt very different and uncomfortable now.

After dinner, we went to an old Irish pub that was apparently a traditional police bar and known for being the place where everyone coming to DC for police week went. The place was literally overflowing with people. It was so packed that we couldn't even get in the front door. I did look inside and could see American flags hanging from the tavern walls. There was rock-and-roll music playing, and there was a sergeant on the stage singing while in full uniform. His uniform shirt was untucked, and I don't believe he had his gun belt on. But he was holding a bottle of booze while trying to slur the words to whatever song was playing. Almost everyone in the bar had a badge either on his or her belt or hanging from a chain around his or her neck. I think it was the most embarrassing and unprofessional scene I've ever witnessed. The group disappeared inside. I told Aaron that I would hang out outside and declined anything to drink. It was about midnight when I saw Aaron next, and I told him that I was going to catch a cab and head back to the hotel. He seemed disappointed that I wasn't into it, but I knew on so many levels that I didn't belong there. We ended up both leaving and walking around the US Capitol Building and Capitol Mall area. It was a really warm night, and the moon shone brightly on the Capitol dome. I couldn't wait to meet up with "my people" the next day.

Aaron ended up sleeping in and missed the conference. I headed out early the next morning and met up with Anthony, a lieutenant from North Carolina who wrote for the first book. It felt so good to finally connect with someone I could relate to. The session I facilitated about coming out on the job had 150 gay and lesbian cops in the room. Although I had never met any of them, I immediately felt more connected and that we shared something in common than I did the night before with people I actually knew. The crowd ranged in age from early twenties to late fifties. They were there from twenty-five different states and five different countries.

I was amazed when I asked, "How many of you are out at work?" It looked like everyone raised his or her hand. I was amazed and confused both by the number of people who were out in their departments and about why they had come to a session on coming out at work. I quickly abandoned all of my plans for the session and moved on. "What was it like for you coming out at work?" We spent the better part of two hours sharing stories about coming out and being out at work. I saw myself in so many of the officers who shared their experiences. It made little difference if the department was in a small town in Iowa or a precinct in New York. The fear, intimidation, and shame people experienced was all the same. Coming out, no matter how old you are or where you are from, takes real courage and becomes a unique, major milestone in your life. When gay people meet for the first time, I've found that the exchange of coming out stories is almost always a part of that introductory conversation. I think because we feel so isolated and so alone for so long, the exchange of coming-out stories helps us find commonality and connection. It was at that moment that I realized why I felt such a disconnection from my travel companions. I ended up spending almost my entire week with Anthony and some new friends from the conference, and I left Aaron and the rest of group behind.

One of my most memorable moments in DC was sitting on the steps of the United States Supreme Court Building waiting for the California Supreme Court to announce its decision about same-sex marriage. Tony and I were married in Canada in 2006, where same-sex marriage has been legal for some time. However, our marriage was not legally recognized in California or by the federal government, so we could not take advantage of any of the some 1,100 benefits associated with legal matrimony. I knew the decision was going to be announced that morning, so I ventured out by myself and sat in the best place I could think of in DC to read a decision that had a direct effect on my own personal civil rights.

I've enjoyed a position of privilege as a white male my entire life. I watched the civil rights movement unfold as a spectator, but now for the first time, I was really feeling like I had a stake in this decision. If the California Supreme Court ruled that same-sex couples were entitled to marry, then under California state law, my marriage to Tony would be considered legal and with the same standing as if we were married in California. This decision had both tangible and intangible implications. When Tony and I made the decision to get married in Canada, we did so because we wanted our marriage to be real and legal. And even though we knew at the time that California would not recognize it, having that certificate was important. So having our marriage recognized in our home state was important to us and particularly to me. Not having the right to marry who I loved in my own state showed me for the first time what inequality feels like. It was really the first time as an out gay man that I felt I was not in a position with privilege.

My phone beeped with a text message. I opened the message and began to read the 172-page decision. Here are two of the most important paragraphs from that case

> "In light of the fundamental nature of the substantive rights embodied in the right to marry—and their central importance to an individual's opportunity to live a happy, meaningful, and satisfying life as a full member of society—the California Constitution properly must be interpreted to guarantee this basic civil right to all individuals and couples, without regard to their sexual orientation. It is true, of course, that as an historical matter in this state marriage always has been limited to a union between a man and a woman. Tradition alone, however, generally has not been viewed as a sufficient justification for perpetuating, without examination, the restriction or denial of a fundamental constitutional right ..." (*In re Marriage Case – Six consolidated appeals, p. 66*)

> "Accordingly, we conclude that the right to marry, as embodied in article I, sections 1 and 7 of the California Constitution, guarantees same-sex couples the same substantive constitutional rights as opposite-sex couples to choose one's life partner and enter with that person into a committed, officially recognized, and protected family relationship that enjoys all of the constitutionally based incidents of marriage." (*In re Marriage Case – Six consolidated appeals, p. 79*)

I stared up at the US Supreme Court Building and at the four words inscribed above the massive columns, "EQUAL JUSTICE UNDER LAW" and felt a sense of victory and great joy.

This decision was important for a number of reasons, not the least of which is that it established marriage as a civil right. It also defeated the idea that tradition has any bearing on one's right to marry. Of course, this case wasn't the first to create a change of "traditional marriage." A marriage between two people of different races was not permitted before state courts began striking down that prohibition on many of the same grounds as California's Supreme Court had just done with same-sex marriage.

I was elated and called Tony at his school immediately. It felt so good. Same-sex marriage ceremonies began in California on June 17, 2008. But there was also a proposition (Proposition 8) coming up on the following November ballot that proposed to rewrite California's Constitution to recognize only marriages between a man and a woman. Tony and I decided that we wanted to make sure our marriage was made valid in case this proposition passed. On September 30, 2008, we went to the Sonoma County Clerk's Office dressed in formal attire and escorted by our witness. We filled out the application and wrote a check for the license. The clerk asked, "Are you going to exchange rings?" Tony said, "Yes, we've done this before." The clerk said, "Wait a minute, are you already married? You can't get remarried in California." That's when we learned that our marriage certificate issued in Canada was equal to one issued in California and that the law prohibited us from getting remarried in our home state. Although disappointed, we left feeling happy and equal.

For someone who grew up thinking that being married and happy would never be possible as a gay man, my marriage to Tony has been truly wonderful. I've always done better living with someone else, but knowing that Tony is there when I come home and to feel his arms wrapped around me gives me such comfort, happiness, and a feeling of love that it's hard to imagine life alone. We are each our own person with our own interests, but life has been so much better having someone to share the celebrations and disappointments with. I enjoy going to watch Tony play tennis, which is his passion, and he enjoys coming to hear me speak. We live in a family-oriented neighborhood where everyone knows one another and where Tony and I are accepted and feel included. We attend birthday parties and all come together as a neighborhood for a Fourth of July barbecue each year. What a great feeling it is to be included equally. Marriage matters, and while not every gay person may decide to make this kind of personal commitment, having the right to do so with the person you love is of monumental importance. I love being married and I love what I have with Tony.

In the months that followed, I watched the effort to pass Proposition 8 mount. I saw my own church, the Catholic Church, join hands with the Mormons to fund most of the "Yes On Proposition 8" campaign. The television ads made me furious. Although I was spared any hate about being gay from the pulpit while growing up, I was hearing it clearly now as an out adult. Under Pope Benedict, the Catholic Church seemed to be retreating to a more hateful position. At the same time the pope and many American bishops were speaking out about the evils of same-sex marriage, they were also trying to cover up decades of sexual abuse both in America and all over the world. The level of hypocrisy was too much, and so I sent the following letter to the Bishop of the Oakland Diocese where I was confirmed.

> November 22, 2008
> Bishop Vigneron,
> I am writing to share my disappointment and disgust with the Catholic Church over its hypocrisy as evidenced by the recent activism in supporting discrimination through Proposition 8. Watching church leaders like yourself as well as the archbishop of San Francisco preach hate from the altar weakens my heart. And this from an organization that has a documented history of covering up thousands of molestations and sexual abuse cases for which its own anointed leaders were direct participants.
>
> How can you call yourself a loving man of God and preach Christ's golden rule of love when you advocate hate for gay and lesbian people? Certainly a man of your intelligence would be able to discern the separation of church and state in this issue. Clearly, Proposition 8 would have no impact on the Catholic Church or its doctrines. The sacrament of marriage and all of the tenants of marriage you describe in your website letter

would remain perfectly intact no matter how the laws in California recognize marriage.

My interest in this issue is deep. I was raised in the Catholic Church, served as an altar boy, and was confirmed by one of your predecessors at St. Monica's in Moraga. I happen to be gay and, unlike so many other current and former Catholics I know, I was never conflicted with my faith. In fact, my faith in God is as strong today as it ever has been. What is missing for me is faith in and any allegiance with the man-made organization known as the Catholic Church.

What has happened in the man-made organization that lead my faith for many years conflicts deeply with everything I ever learned from this same organization. Fortunately, the acts of hypocrisy and hate I've observed and the discriminatory words I've read that you and other Catholic leaders have written have not weakened my faith in God. But clearly the human leaders of this organization represent values that I do not. Allying myself with an organization that has obstructed justice, covered up abuses, and that promotes discrimination and hate is not one that I want anything to do with.

I'm confident that if I had done such things in the name of the Catholic Church, you would have advocated for my excommunication. I feel exactly the same way about your church, and I say "yours" because I can no longer call it "mine" and still stand by the word of God. The preaching of hate and advocacy for discrimination is so hypocritical and sinful that I will no longer call myself a Catholic. What I have witnessed has given me cause to excommunicate the man-made organization known as the Catholic Church from my life.

I'm confident that I am not the first gay man who used

to consider himself a Catholic that you've heard from. I urge you to really search your heart and to think about the positions and values you are representing. Do they reflect the values of a loving God? Are you leading the church from a position based on faith or from direction you receive from another man? Perhaps the future will enable you to consider God's love for everyone as a being he created and to accept all of his gay children as equals. Hopefully this acceptance will stop the preaching of discrimination and hate from the altar and thus stop the hypocrisy. I pray that this will ease the hearts of so many people I know who live in shame, guilt, and conflict.

I look forward to your response, and I pray that you will emerge as a leader for what is right in God's eyes rather than from what you have been told is right.

Proposition 8 invalidated my marriage in California. The following March, the California Supreme Court ruled that same-sex marriages performed in California between June 17, 2008, and November 4, 2008, (the day Proposition 8 passed) were still recognized, but that Proposition 8 was passed legally and in compliance with the California State Constitution. What the court didn't explain was about those marriages—like mine—that were performed out of state and legally recognized before Proposition 8. Remember, we tried to get married in California, but the state law at the time prohibited us from doing so. Senator Mark Leno, a brilliant and highly successful legislator who happens to be gay, authored a bill which clarified that same-sex marriages performed outside of California prior to the passage of Proposition 8 are recognized and legal as a marriage. The governor, much to my surprise, signed the bill, and—once again—our marriage was legally recognized in California.

I've become much more outspoken about a variety of civil rights issues related to the LGBT community. While I still consider the focus of my work to be on supporting LGBT law enforcement personnel, the greater arena of LGBT civil rights relates directly to gay cops. Whether it is the military's Don't Ask, Don't Tell policy or the need for national employment protection, I think everyone in our community needs to be involved and engaged in our push for equality and achieving the same civil rights as those with privilege.

One of the real highlights in my life after coming out is my work with the Matthew Shepard Foundation. Judy Shepard has been alongside me since my coming-out journey began in 2001. Tony and I have been active in the work of the Matthew Shepard Foundation since we first met in 2004, and we've been fortunate to have made some incredible friends along the way. The commonality of our struggle first to come out and then to find a place of equality is a powerful force in creating a unique community that is gaining large numbers of straight allies by the day. I've shared Matt's story and the viciousness of his hate crime murder with everyone who will listen.

Matthew Shepard dreamed of someday changing the world. I believe he has done so in ways he could never have imagined. Certainly one of the most visible changes was the passage of the Matthew Shepard and James Byrd, Jr. Hate Crimes Prevention Act in October 2009. Since Matt was killed, Judy and Dennis Shepard have worked tirelessly to get federal hate crimes law changed to include sexual orientation. The passage of this act was considered to be the first and one of the most significant advances for gay rights in this century. Many foundations established after someone dies have a shelf life and then fade away. While it hasn't always been easy, the Matthew Shepard Foundation has grown up and is now focused on education and prevention. This work is important because no hate crime law will actually prevent a hate crime from happening. They are valuable only for dealing with those responsible for hate crimes, but after the victim has already suffered. The key to preventing hate crimes is to change the hearts and minds of potential offenders through education and awareness. The foundation's work now is really even more important than ever, and I'm very proud to be a member of the board of directors.

Coming out is not a process that happens on just one day, one week, or even one year. It happens continuously, sometimes daily, for the rest of your life. Fortunately, it's not as torturous or frightening as time goes on, but if you think you will be able to say, "I'm gay" once and be done with it, you are quite wrong. While I never imagined sharing my most intimate secrets in a book, I certainly never could hear myself talking about being gay and married to man on the radio. In 2009, Tony and I were invited by Sheridan Gold and Dr. Dianna Grayer to be interviewed on their radio show called *Living Proof*. It's a show that airs as part of a weekly LGBT program called *Outbeat Radio* on KRCB Radio in Santa Rosa. Tony agreed to do the show, and we had a blast! They say practice makes perfect, so I guess if you talk about being gay enough, it does in fact get easier—and that it did.

In fact, I was so excited about doing the show that I contacted Robin Pressman, the programming director for KRCB, and I pitched an idea for an LGBT youth show. Tony agreed to be a cohost, and we began working on a pilot. It took several months to get things together, but in August of 2009, we completed a one-hour pilot show and presented it to the station. Tony discovered that he didn't mind being interviewed as a guest but really didn't like being a host at all. I told him that I wanted to move forward, and, of course, he was entirely supportive. I ended up teaming with two other guys from the station to create a new show called *Outbeat Now!* with my segment *Outbeat Youth* being half of the show. I created a website (www.outbeatyouth.com) and corresponding pages on all the social networking sites. I've interviewed Joe Solmonese from the Human Rights Campaign, Jon Barrett from the *Advocate* magazine, and some amazing young people who were able to share their own coming-out stories on the radio for the first time. In May of 2010, I was able to produce a one-hour special for the radio all about how LGBT law enforcement personnel have become more visible within the profession.

My work with the Matthew Shepard Foundation, our local LGBT youth group Positive Images, the radio show, and of course the book satisfied a calling I felt for activism. And while I realize that being so visible may not be for everyone, I do feel that everyone in the LGBT community has a responsibility to do something. So many men and women fought hard and sacrificed much for the liberties and civil rights we have today. They helped make coming out easier for you and me, and I believe we owe it to their legacy to continue the fight. Find a cause, an effort, a topic, a belief that you have passion for and give to it. Maybe it's a momentary contribution, or maybe it's a donation of your time and talent. Whatever it is, give something back to the cause.

The writing of the first book became a platform for a number of other projects associated with the book's website. I started recording and posting monthly podcasts on a variety of issues related to coming out and gay rights. Some of the content from those podcasts is included the second part of this book for your review. One of my goals from the very beginning of the project was to develop a scholarship program to support LGBT students in basic law enforcement training programs. There is nothing like it in the nation except for some local scholarships offered by larger agencies for their own students. The idea is to not only support future LGBT members of law enforcement, but to make the presence of LGBT law enforcement personnel visible. We have been within the ranks of law enforcement from the beginning but are only now becoming more visible beyond the rare and token exception. I know from what I've learned since coming out that there is on average one gay student in every one of our classes and likely more. It takes tremendous courage to come out in that type of training situation, but having students come out in the academy setting is exactly what we need to combat the widespread homophobia that still exists within the profession.

In March of 2009, Out To Protect Incorporated was officially formed as a tax-exempt, nonprofit corporation. A good friend, who is also an attorney, donated his time to help us put the corporation together. It took just about one year to get the 501(c)(3) tax exempt status from the Internal Revenue Service, but we got it and immediately began raising money. I put together a board of directors that includes Tony, Damien from the academy, and my good friend Ben from San Francisco Police Department. We established the following mission statement for the program:

> *Create a greater awareness of the gay, lesbian, bisexual,*
> *and transgender professionals working in law enforcement*
> *and to support those pursuing a law enforcement career.*

In June of 2010, we awarded our first scholarship to a young lesbian student from our academy in Napa. Putting this program together has definitely had its challenges, not the least of which has been raising money in a bad economy that could rival the Great Depression. It's also been tough advertising the scholarship opportunity and getting applications. But we are in no rush and will continue to push for donations. Our goal is to award two $1,000 scholarships in June and December each year. The profits from this book will all be dedicated to supporting the scholarship program, so you can feel good as you read on.

I've also tried to create content and resources on the book's website to support LGBT law enforcement personnel and our straight allies. I've focused primarily on supporting closeted officers by offering connection and resources. My intent is to continue growing the site in the future, as I now consider this area of training and teaching the most important part of my personal mission as a teacher. Being a teacher is what I have always enjoyed most about my job.

Whether it was training in the police department or teaching part time at the academy, being in the classroom is truly my passion. Let me take you back to what's happened at the police academy and college since coming out. Word about my first book spread quickly but quietly to students and staff. The first incident was actually pretty funny and happened while a student was making his cross-cultural research project presentation. We require police academy cadets to select a culture based on nationality, religion, disability, race, or sexual orientation that they are unfamiliar with. The choice is the student's, but in all cases, they must immerse themselves in the culture by visiting a cultural center or event, and they must complete three face-to-face interviews with members of the culture. The students work together in groups of two or three and present back their findings to the rest of the class. So at the time this happened, I started writing the book and had a website about the book up online, but my name was nowhere on the site. I wasn't out to my students or most of the staff, although I didn't cover up or hide who I was. Even though I had been out for almost two years at the time, as the director of the police academy, I was still getting comfortable with being gay in this role.

I was sitting in the room with Damien, with whom I've team-taught this project for ten years. We were listening to a presentation about the gay community. One of the students began talking about a book he read as part of the research he did for the project. He described the book as being about gay police officers and how he read a story about one that made him sad. He described how this officer had been hiding who he really was for twenty-five years and then finally came out. I couldn't help but to raise my hand and ask him the title of the book. He said, "*Coming Out from Behind the Badge.*" I turned to Damien and whispered, "Wow, amazing that he read a book that hasn't even been written yet." It was funny, but it made me squirm.

Later that year, a student who I suspected was gay also found out about the book and approached me directly about it. He also asked about the release event and where it was going to be. Of course I told him and invited him to come. He seemed to know a great deal about the Castro area of San Francisco but then proceeded to make fun of me and the book to his classmates. He was not a very popular student with his peers, and I understood the dynamics of internalized homophobia that was likely in play with him. It still made me angry nonetheless, though, and I definitely let him know about it. I never heard from him again.

In the months following the release of the book, on several occasions, instructors on our staff walked into my office with a copy of the book and asked for my signature. I never got used to that both because of the surprise at who it was that bought a copy and the randomness of it all. It was the same feeling I had of coming out to each of the individuals I had told but without the control of when and where. Of course I knew that anyone who read the book would know all of the secrets I shared in it, but it was nevertheless still awkward.

On several occasions during these comings-out of sorts, I had instructors share with me that they have a gay son, nephew, or stepson. In one particular case, a guy I had taught with for twenty years and whom I had to discipline for telling a homophobic joke walked into my office, sat down, and said, "I read your book." I replied with caution, "Oh yeah?" He said, "It was excellent. Now I understand." It was clear that they were caring and supportive of me and that I had completely underestimated how my story would be received. I think we are conditioned to expect the worst based on stories we've heard and read about with others. What I've learned is that is all about the person you are and the foundations of the relationships you've developed with people that really determines how you will be received.

In 2008, the college reorganized, and I became responsible for all career training programs that the college offers, including the police academy. My teaching partner, Damien, became the new academy director. It was a very new role for me, with much greater visibility at the college-wide level. It also allowed me to continue teaching in the police academy—but now really as a teacher not the academy director. It felt much more comfortable and more distant from the political pressure I was feeling from the homophobia that I know exists in our local law enforcement community. There isn't another out male law enforcement officer in the two counties we directly serve. And I know from talking with friends who work in different departments in this region that it would be very difficult to come out in these agencies and to be successful. Although I never once heard a negative word about being gay at any point from anyone within this law enforcement community, I do know that there was a lot of conversation going on behind my back. But whatever it was, it never impacted me or interfered with my position at the college.

Coming out to the rest of the college has been a process of opportunity, but of course, it has not been without some interesting events. I knew my boss for the twenty-five years I had been at the college, but she didn't really know me personally, and I had never formally come out to her. It wasn't because of fear that I didn't come out, but it just wasn't necessary because we didn't work that closely together. At the same time I assumed my new position, the other dean position was filled by a faculty member named Faye who was promoted from within the ranks for the faculty. I knew who she was but didn't really know her, and she didn't really know me. I always really liked her and looked forward to us working together.

That fall, I arranged for Judy Shepard to come to Napa to attend a reading of *The Laramie Project* in commemoration of the tenth year since Matt was murdered. This event was one of only two she attended that fall in memory of Matt. It was a huge community event that we held at the Napa Opera House downtown. Our then college president Chris McCarthy participated as a reader, and much of the college administration attended. Of course, Tony was at my side and helped me with the logistics that night. Aside from Damien, no one attending that night had ever met Tony, so with each introduction of Tony came a "coming out" to that person. As people started to arrive, I saw Faye come into the room with a woman. I walked up and introduced Tony as my partner. She replied, "And this is Dawn, my partner." Oh my, I wonder if our boss realized what she was doing when she promoted both of us at the same time!

If you have heard or read *The Laramie Project*, you know that it is a very powerful and emotional play. After the first act, there wasn't a dry eye in the house. Tony and I were sitting near the front row. Everyone got up to stretch and to wipe away the tears. Tony and I stood, hugged, and kissed right in front of the entire theater. I thought to myself, *Well, if you haven't figured it out yet, there's no hope for any of you.* That was a pivotal night for me. By simply introducing Tony as my partner, I was able to come out to just about everyone I worked closely with. It felt seamless and completely normal, as it should be.

In July 2009, I started to take a new approach with my academy classes. Since first coming out, I had a dozen or more former students e-mail, call, or stop by the academy to visit and to come out to me. It really made me realize that we do, in fact, have gay students in every class, and just like any other minority in the law enforcement profession, they need a role model. We've always tried to present a faculty that is diverse and that presents a variety of role models for students of all types. However, we have no out gay or lesbian instructors. Given the fact that I was responsible for teaching all of the human relations and workplace harassment classes, it made even more sense for me to share all of who I am from the start. My hope was to make it easier for that gay student who was there hiding in fear of being found out or of being rejected by his peers and the staff. I talked with Damien about coming out to classes on the first day I meet them and shared with him my intent. He was of course completely supportive.

I meet the classes on the third day of their academy. There are usually about fifty students in the room, most of whom are still very nervous and uncertain about the military rigor of the academy. I walk in the room with my wedding ring in my pocket and explain that I will be covering human relations topics that include discussions about biases, stereotypes, prejudice, and hate. I go on to talk some about my background with the intent of creating a stereotype in their minds. It goes something like this.

I've worked in law enforcement for the last thirty years

and with three different departments, my last as a deputy chief. I've been teaching here at the academy for twenty-five years, starting with the academy's third graduating class. I've had the honor of teaching just about every topic in the academy except first aid and CPR. I was never good at that. I taught firearms and chemical agents for ten years, and I wrote the book on chemical agents that you will be using in the academy. I've also taught impact weapons, use of force, and testified as an expert in both areas. I have a master's degree in education, a bachelor's degree in business, and I am a POST master instructor.

I go on a bit more, but you get the idea. I then ask the class if they have anything else they would like to know about me.

Since we are going to be talking about biases and stereotypes, based on what I have said, what assumptions might you make about me?

That almost always prompts the question, "Sir, do you have a family?" I then ask why they would ask that question and usually get a comment back about not seeing a wedding ring. I take the ring out of my pocket and put it on my left ring finger. I ask then about what the ring tells you. The conversation leads me to being able to say that I am married to a man named Tony. There is always a combination of smiles and some surprise or even shock. But in all cases, I've been well received, and it feels so great to be able to share all of me, just like many of our other instructors do.

What this disclosure has led to throughout the academy is the ability to have open and honest conversation about sexual orientation and what my experience in law enforcement has been. I know absolutely that I've made at least three students more comfortable after finding out later in the academy that they are gay. In fact, in one class, there were three gay students in the same class! The students appreciate the honesty and the ability to ask their questions without having to worry about stepping on eggshells. While you would think that young people coming into the academy today would have already been exposed to gay and lesbian people, I'm always surprised by the number of students who claim that I am the first gay person they've met in person.

I would never have imagined what this coming-out process would have lead to later in my career. Well, of course we continue to require the cross-cultural research project, and one of the groups from the first class I came out to that selected the gay community for their project asked me if I would take them to the Castro and show them around. They said that they wanted to meet other gay police officers. So the next thing I knew, I was meeting a group of six academy cadets at the Muni train station located directly under the huge rainbow flag that flies over the Castro. Several of these students had never been to San Francisco, let alone to one of the largest gay communities in the world. If you know my story from the first book, you might recall the terror and fear I experienced the first time I visited the Castro. Now, here I was showing a group of presumably straight students around.

I can say only that it was an incredible experience. We visited the gay bookstore, Harvey Milk's apartment and location where his camera store was located, the Human Rights Campaign store, and then we sat and talked over lunch for two hours. A couple of friends from San Francisco Police Department joined us and shared their stories, as well. They all took pictures and returned to the academy with a new understanding of the gay community that they never would have learned researching the topic on the Internet. Since this first trip, I've taken groups of students and anyone else from their class who wants to go to the Castro as part of their research. In every case, questions and discussion about whether it is a choice, as well as other discussions about religion, family, and how to connect with a gay family member who was rejected years ago becomes a totally moving experience for everyone at the table.

Perhaps the most amazing experience related to this project happened at this year's gay pride parade in San Francisco. The president of the San Francisco Police Department Pride Alliance, Lieutenant Lea Militello, periodically meets with me and our students while visiting the Castro. This time, she invited all of us to march with the San Francisco Police Department Pride Alliance in the pride parade. I never thought our students would do it, but they did! So there we all were on the morning of the parade—Tony, my good friends from San Francisco

Police Department, four of my students, and me. They were so amazing and supportive. And what a presentation they did for their classmates. Now that was an immersion into the culture!

What Tony has told me throughout our time together continues to be absolutely true. "People will be as comfortable with you as you are with yourself." As I have come out to more and more people at work, to my students, and even over an FM radio station, it gets easier each time. And as the number of people who accept me grows, I feel less concerned about those I might have met who don't. Their opinions about me never should have mattered, but the reality is that they once did. Now I can say with a reasonable level of confidence that they no longer do. I am who I am, take it or leave it, but I'm not spending one bit of energy worrying about what anyone thinks.

# Blue Before Pink—
# Peter Thoshinksy

I'm writing this for the guy far into his career, struggling in a world that sees him as straight, who is looking for stories that relate to them.

If you were born in the last twenty-five to thirty years, you may not be able to relate to my story. The generational gap from 1975 to 1995 is, after all, not a simple twenty years. It is much more than that. There has been a sea of change in our society since I became a police officer. It is a sea of change fueled by the Internet—a device so profound and earth changing that when I write the word *Internet* in a story such as this, I find myself forced to place the word in capitalizations as if it were a proper noun.

If you are gay and were born in the last twenty-five to thirty years, I have something to say to you. Listen carefully. Your rights, your acceptance, are fragile. Relish these times when you can express your sexuality, at least in the "civilian world," without derision, comment, or persecution. We are at a crossroads not just in America, but in the world. Today across the globe, billions of persons stand to persecute you. Don't take your freedom for granted. Do you remember Ronald Reagan's inauguration? Good.

Let's get this straight, excuse the pun. You, the reader, and I are two of the straightest-acting guys in the world. No one, not a soul, suspects. Like me, you are on your sixth issued bulletproof vest and twenty-second pair of patrol boots. God, I can't fucking believe I'm gay! Me of all fucking people! I don't look gay. I don't act gay. I'm not a pussy or a pervert. I'm not a nerd. I hang out with guys, doing guy things. No one suspects I'm gay. Hell, even I can't believe I'm gay!

I'm fifty-one years of age. I have been a San Francisco police officer for twenty-eight years, the last twenty as a patrol sergeant as well as a tactical sergeant. Two years ago, I came out of the closet.

***Gaymath;***
***Pronunciation: \□\□gāimath\***
***Function: verb***
***Etymology: Modern English gaymath,* homosexual \<gay men\> b: of, relating to, or used by homosexuals \<the gay rights movement\> \<a gay bar\>math, of, relating to, the study of mathematics.**
**1.To calculate, or to apply the calculation, to a known population of humans to determine the ratio or content of heterosexuals versus homosexuals with a group or crowd, usually as a method to provide psychological comfort to closeted gay persons. 2. To apply a ratio derived from the Kinsey report on human sexuality, usually as a ratio of 1:10, to determine the sexual practices of a group or groups. Ex; I can calculate that there are 10 gay men in the business meeting of one hundred persons by dividing 100 by 10. (Data From Alfred Kinsey's Studies, 1996)**

Sniper training, Camp Parks, California. I remember the day very well, although I don't remember the exact date. I was in my early forties. I was walking back from downrange, an assault rifle, gear, and magazines all in their place in my cool ninja SWAT outfit. Around me, another twenty of my tactical team buddies, dressed just like me, were ready for urban battle.

This is just one third of the team. There are sixty of us. Once again, I did the math. Is it one in ten, or should I use one in five? Or was it just me out here? Damn, I was really starting to dislike myself. This isn't good.


I'm not just another team member here; I'm the sergeant running the team. In fact, "running" the team is a slight understatement. Over the last ten years, I have been a strict disciplinarian, a stickler for standards. Our team has evolved significantly over the last decade. We have the greatest officers and tactical staff one could ask for. We sometimes work sixteen-hour days when training. Guys, and sometimes a few gals, have worked really hard, and the team has thrived. We have become really good at what we do.

Default is probably as good a reason as any why I have ended up in charge. When I had first joined the specialist team in 1983, we were all expected to get more advanced certifications and become trainers or instructors. I had ended up being a rifle instructor and a sniper as a patrol officer, and it so happened that when I was promoted to sergeant, the current training sergeant was leaving. I got the job. Lucky me. There was a lot of talk back then about liability falling back upon trainers. I realized right away that the amount of exposure I was subject to, both legally and morally, was tremendous. I became driven. I wasn't going to be in charge of training and operations for the specialist team and for the San Francisco Police Department in the "real world" and not be prepared for both the gunfight and the court fight.

I was a ballbuster. It helped that I didn't have a lot of allegiance to any one group in the police department. I was just the sergeant with the fucked-up last name who didn't know one Catholic school from another. The specialist team—like all parts of the SFPD—has an old boy's network, where the Italians take care of Italians, blacks for blacks, Asians for Asians, gays for gays, Irish for Irish, and Latino for Latino. I call these "mafias." The department is full of mafias drawn up along ethnic, cultural, and political lines. It permeates not just the department but the entire city. I wasn't in a mafia. I don't believe in mafias. I simply didn't care. Perform or leave.

I kicked dead wood off the specialist team. I insisted that everyone meet the FBI minimum sniper standards within a year or leave. When they didn't make standards, I forced them off. The reader must understand that I was going against the grain. Fortunately, I had absolute and total backing from my captain, the guy who oversees all of the day-to-day functions of the special operations group. Without him, the specialist team would never have evolved. He backed me because he recognized that the world had changed, and the department faced new challenges. The captain backed me all the way. I kicked guys off the team for failing to attend training. I didn't actually kick them off. I just made them not certified in the weapons system and not eligible for critical incident response. They left on their own. The job isn't for everyone. You give 100 percent or you leave. God bless you.

Then I extended our basic entry course for incoming specialists from three days to two weeks … and then from two weeks to three. The specialist team basic training is built around one concept. Teach them. Once they know how to do something, make them tired. Run them and PT them. Drill them. Teach them some more. Demand perfection. Run them and PT them until they are about as tired as one is after not sleeping for a day and a half and trying to remain alert lying twelve feet away from some barricaded suspect's back bedroom next to pit bull dog turds. Then we see if the candidate can still perform. You would be surprised how many officers have trouble performing some basic mental tasks when fatigued, such as counting backward from one hundred during training, much less forgetting the description of the hostage.

I'm a fitness freak. I was known to eat so much, so often, that people called me Sergeant Sandwich. (Go figure—a gay and overachieving guy being into fitness?) I ran really tough courses. I did everything in my power to make the courses as challenging and realistic as possible. Within a few years, I had been the training coordinator for every active member of the specialist team. I had personally trained each and every one of the then forty-eight and then sixty-man team. Many of these team members eventually moved out of "patrol" and over to the full-time tactical entry teams. Soon, it seemed I had trained every SWAT cop in the city.

Over the next few years, we safely resolved dozens of tactical incidents and hundreds of demonstrations, which in San Francisco are hard core and often violent. I was proving myself as a street sergeant, as a trainer, as a tactical leader, and many times as the tactical platoon commander.

I ended up in this job by circumstances. I wasn't trying to be here.

Yet here I was. And it's a no bullshit job. In this type of job, you can't say, "Well, this isn't life and death," because that's exactly what it is. Life and death. Yours. His. Mine. Someone's. We guard the president. We guard the pope. We guard kings, queens, and foreign heads of state.

Leadership, of course, requires the trust and confidence of those you lead. It can vaporize in an instant. If you make one bad call, make one stupid decision, or God forbid you get someone hurt, that trust is gone. Once that trust is gone, the ability to lead is difficult—maybe even impossible—to regain. As a leader of men, I didn't see my homosexuality as being a benefit.

I was, and still am, a tough boss. There is no other way to put it. I don't play when it comes to this job. I had been the tactical commander when a guy went postal in a high-rise office tower. I had seen how quickly these situations can cost lives if not ended swiftly. I knew then and I know now how murderous one well-armed human being can be in *seconds*. It's very, very serious business, and it requires bold, active, and decisive leadership. Look at Columbine or North Hollywood. Closer to home for me, San Francisco's 101 California Street. Then again in San Francisco at Pine and Franklin Streets, November 1993 when SFPD Patrol Officer and Specialist Team Member James Guelff was cut down by a crazy gunman armed with multiple assault weapons and body armor. It would be a long gun battle resulting in another cop critically shot and responding paramedics injured by long-range rifle fire before the suspect was brought down by a sniper sneaking up on the bad guy's "six." Hesitation and unnecessary delay are deadly when some suspect—or, God forbid, a terrorist—starts playing tag with an AK-47. Because of the double life I felt I was leading, I felt that I was a liar. It felt inherently wrong.

(Hey, teammates, did I mention that I'm gay?)

By 1993, I had taken over as the team executive officer and was responsible for the day-to-day running of the team. During the next few years, for all intents, I ended up as the team lieutenant. The real team lieutenant at that time was absent. The boss spent his on-duty hours attending to his tennis game. I became the face of the specialist team.

(Ahem. By the way, I'm gay.)

When the next lieutenant came along, I got lucky. He was a damned sharp leader and a great cop who was well known and respected. He was a good match for the team. Unlike our previous boss, he took a keen and serious interest in the team. Because of him, the specialist team, along with the tactical SWAT entry teams and EOD teams, stand today as one of the finest special operations groups in the country. Today's SFPD tactical members carry on this dedication, commitment, and excellence in a much more difficult and even more challenging post-9/11 environment.

I had evolved. I had become very much an "alpha male" among "alpha males" in an "alpha male" job. So do you think I wanted anyone to know that I was gay? Here I was, many years later, doing "gay math" on the rifle range. I certainly didn't plan to end up here on the rifle range doing the "gay math" thing trying to figure out who among this cadre of SWAT cops was gay. One in five, divided among sixty, but don't count yourself. Hmmm, maybe one in ten. Split it! One in 7.5. Do I count bisexuals?

Gay math.

I had a plan. I created it sometime back in my teenage years, way back in the seventies—back when the word "gay" was still new to me. Here was my plan. It was really pretty simple. I could jack off and fantasize to whatever I wanted to in my head, but in my life, I was going to stay straight. So long as I never had sex with a guy, I wasn't really gay. This started the "Big Lie" or the "Big Hope" or the "Phase." Take your pick. We all have a name for this period in our young gay lives. I'm sure you, the reader, can relate.

I grew up in San Francisco in the '60s and '70s. You would think that as a gay kid, one couldn't ask for anything better. But in truth, it was just the opposite. While thousands ran away from places like Kansas to San Francisco to come out, I lived in San Francisco and stayed there. I loved San Francisco then and still do today. While it might be easy to move to a new place and make new friends out of strangers as you "come out," the opposite holds true if that same place is where *you* grew up. Move away where? I'm already there, and everyone knows me. I always found it ironic that people were coming to *my* city to "come out" either to total strangers or to fellow queers. I didn't see much risk announcing their homosexuality to strangers. If I told everyone in Seattle I was gay, who the fuck would care? I am a native son. My grandfather came here fleeing the persecution of Jews in Russia in 1911. I already lived in this gay mecca called San Francisco. In my world in the 1970s, gays were the butts of most every joke told in school. I got the message loud and clear. Gays were freaks, pussies, and perverts. I saw the footage from the gay parade. I saw them in town, "ground zero." The nuns of perpetual indulgence weren't scoring too many supporters and certainly not much tolerance. I saw them as a bunch of freaks and fairies! Gay was the last thing a guy wanted to be. Getting your ass kicked in high school was easy enough all on its own.

Besides, even if I wanted to leave the city I loved, I didn't have a "gay city" to run off to. I was already there. I was a young guy. I was getting established and making my way into the adult world. I wanted to fit in. I didn't want to be different. Gay could wait.

The "Big Lie" begins in 1971. I'm twelve. I can name nearly every single boy in my school, but I can barely name a single girl. I am looking for every opportunity to be naked with other guys, usually at the swimming pool, the gym, the locker room, or at sleepovers. It's 11:00 p.m. on a summer night in 1971. Tonight, I'm spending the night at my friend Craig's home. Once again, we are naked. As we had for years, we are naked and trading massages. No sex. We just both knew we enjoyed being naked with each other. Very innocent stuff. I'm not even much into puberty yet. As far as I was concerned, everything was fine in the world. We were just two innocent twelve-year-olds being innocent happy twelve-year-olds. Life is all model airplanes and the San Francisco 49ers.

I was buck naked on top of Craig giving him a shoulder massage. He was naked, too. Suddenly, I noticed that Craig seemed to be looking back over his shoulder, but not at me. His sister had walked in, something I didn't notice and I wouldn't grasp for several seconds as I continued my very innocent naked massage. Craig was speechless. I was clueless. I had my back to the door. That's when I first heard *that* word, exclaimed loud and clear in the sleeping house. It was a word I had never heard. It had more syllables than any word I had heard, and my friend's sister was making sure *everyone* in the house could hear every single one of those syllables.

She yelled it over and over. "*HOMO-SEX-UALS, HOMO-SEX-UALS!*" She yelled it as four distinct words. "Homo. Sex. You. Wills." They were from South Carolina and said it with a southern accent. She then bolted from the room, still screaming that word and waking up the entire neighborhood. "Homo! Sex! You! Wills! Homo! Sex! You! Wills!" Within seconds, my life changed. Craig's sister went running to tell their dad. My friend had a terrified look on his face as he put his clothes on as fast as he could. I sat their naked asking my friend what that word meant—and what in the hell was wrong? He wouldn't answer, but his look said it all. For some reason, we were in deep shit. I kept asking what was wrong, and what the heck was his sister yelling about? And what in the hell was that stupid word? God, I hate girls!

Craig's father was awakened by her screaming that word, and we were both called upstairs. Craig's father was, fortunately enough, a psychiatrist whose practice focused on children and adolescents. That probably saved us a beating, but it didn't do much to explain to me his older sister's panic or end my total and absolute confusion as to what we had done wrong. My friend's dad patiently explained to us that homosexual play between boys was normal. I sat their trying to figure out what that had to do with giving Craig a naked massage. Who was he talking about? Craig's dad droned on about sex this and homosexual that. I sat there wondering when we were going to find out what his sister was yelling about. The lecture ended. My friend had clearly understood the conversation. I didn't have a clue. Pressed for an explanation, Craig made it clear that what we had been doing was wrong, and we couldn't ever do it again. Except for one more time, we never did. That final time was a few weeks later. Upstairs in his bedroom, we had taken off all our clothes and were just admiring one another when his dad walked in. I had just enough time to jump behind the open door and the wall and hide. I was peeking out through the crack between the wall and the door. Craig calmly dressed and chatted with his dad. His dad never knew that I was there, naked and terrified, hiding behind the door scared to be caught doing that "homosexual" thing. I hid for five minutes as Craig and his dad talked. That door I hid behind that day should have been a closet door, because I stayed there for another thirty years.

Craig moved to a different neighborhood not long after. I saw him a few times, but things had changed. He started hanging with a tough crowd. At sixteen, he was arrested and convicted for gay bashing and robbing a guy in the Castro. He eventually got married and had kids. I looked him up a few months ago on the Internet. At forty-nine, he committed suicide, leaving behind two boys. I wasn't really surprised. I cry even today as I write this.

About this same time, the "Phase" came along. The book *Everything You Always Wanted to Know about Sex but Were Afraid to Ask* suddenly appeared in my home. It was no doubt left by my parents for me to find. I found that word again—homosexuals. The book explained that sex play between boys was a "normal phase" that all boys go through and eventually grow out of. So I was just in a phase. Cool. I'm going through a phase. I don't recall the book discussing homosexuality in any other way. I wish it had. I wasn't a homosexual. I was just going through a phase. No mention was made of the fact that this "phase" might not go away.

Like a drowning boy, I grasped and held onto the "phase" to stay afloat.

The phase continued. I played sports. I partied. I drank and smoked. I played football. I dated girls. I had sex with girls in the backseats of cars. I was horny enough that anything related to sex got me hard, although orgasm frequently needed hot fantasies of guys to finish the act. I searched a popular mens' magazine known for its "forums," occasionally finding solace in some hot homosexual or bisexual story confirming that at least someone out there was just like me. To me, jacking off was certainly all about guys. I promised myself that I would stop thinking about guys as I jacked off. I even promised I would stop jacking off! I made a lot of promises then. Years went by. I was sure hoping this phase would end soon. The phase didn't end in high school. It didn't end in college. By twenty, I had resigned myself to the fact that this phase thing promised to me as a straw to grasp on to by Miss Xavier Hollander was, at least in my case, a big lie. The fact that I had jacked off to Xavier Hollander's other writings containing homosexual stories should have been a clue.

So the "phase" had ended. Now it was just a "big lie." I will never have sex with guys. So long as I never have sex with guys, I'm not gay. I will never tell anyone. It is secret, and I'm taking it to my grave. Everyone knows that if you don't suck dick you aren't gay. Done deal. Life is hard enough.

In the fall of 1974, a friend of mine told me that the San Francisco Police Department had a radio car and cop stuff on display over at the Stonestown Mall. They had even landed the police helicopter. We wandered down. Among all the neat cop toys was a booth. The SFPD had a police cadet program. They were recruiting. I joined the cadet program simply because I had nothing else to do. I was bored. Besides, the SFPD was in the news a lot in those days. This was the tail end of the days of police stations in San Francisco getting bombed and cops being ambushed.

During this period, a black school superintendent was assassinated in Oakland by a group calling itself the SLA. Patty Hearst was coming into the news. The "Zodiac" was a household name and well on its way to legend, and the word "zebra" would become a commonly used word in San Francisco within a short while. The "Zebra Killers," as they became known, were a cult of radical blacks Muslims who were randomly murdering, sometimes by abduction and horrific torture, innocent people chosen simply for being white. A fifteen-year-old friend of mine, a fellow police cadet but in street clothes, was standing on a street corner about a mile from my home as he waited for the bus. A car pulled up. A man got out. He shot my friend eight times in the stomach point blank with a .380 automatic. My friend somehow survived, but several more people that night were not so lucky. And the SFPD seemed to be right in the middle of everything. The SFPD was in the evening news and in the morning paper.

For some reason, I fit in well as a cadet, and it would become an anchor for me as I struggled over the next few years. I don't know why, but I was really good at leading and organizing. I quickly found myself running a lot of things. What can I say? I got lucky and stumbled upon something that suited me perfectly and something I enjoyed. I was just learning that I had a knack for leading. My mom committed suicide when I was fifteen, the morning after Thanksgiving. With just me and my sister at home, my mom shot herself with a .38. It left me devastated. Everything after the moment of that gunshot became either a "before Mom" or "after Mom" moment. It separates my childhood from my adulthood like a guillotine. I never thought as a child again. I now envision my life as a ceramic bowl dropped on the ground. The pieces are all glued back together. You have to look hard and know where to look to see any of the cracks. The bowl still works, but it's not the same. Like that dropped ceramic bowl, I was never, ever the same again.

My older brother had already left for college the year before and stayed away except to show up stoned at Thanksgiving. By 1976, my sister had moved off to college, leaving me virtually alone in the house. My father, a terribly mean and narcissist individual, ignored my mom's suicide and just went on with his life and found a new girlfriend. Dad rarely came home.

I was contemplating suicide every waking moment. I had come very close several times. Once I had crawled into the back of my closet with my .22 rifle. Among the clothes hanging in the closet, wedged up in a corner, I sat staring into the barrel of that .22 rifle. I tried to work up the nerve. I stared at that little black hole forever. I didn't do it. I didn't do it because I decided that I could do it tomorrow. I decided to do something that I tell every person I meet at work who is thinking of committing suicide. Wait until tomorrow. I could wait one more day. I can always kill myself tomorrow. I look back on my life. Those days were the most black and the most painful times I have ever experienced. Those black days also taught me that I could overcome anything. They didn't kill me. They came close, but I came out stronger.

In the meantime, I hurt. A lot. I was in so much emotional pain that I could barely get out of bed. By sixteen, I was on my own doing whatever I wanted. That meant smoking as much pot and doing as many drugs as I could. I wasn't doing it to be cool. I wasn't exposed to drugs. I sought them out. I just wanted the pain of my mom's suicide to go away. I was trying to make it through to tomorrow.

That is, except for one night a week. One night each week, I had the police cadet meeting, and I morphed from hippie stoner to the good kid. One night a week, I couldn't get high. As I was given more and more responsibility as a cadet leader, that one night a week became three nights a week. Three nights I couldn't drink or smoke or do drugs. It saved my life.

I had two girlfriends in high school. I had no trouble acting straight because I wasn't acting. I felt straight. I wanted to be straight. I looked straight. That meant dating, or at least trying to get laid. With a couple of girls, I succeeded. I was so incredibly horny at that age that for a long while I believed that I had fucked myself straight. Straight sex was great, or at least good enough, and it made up for the guilt from my masturbation fantasies. Well, sort of. The truth was that I was hoping to somehow have sex with some guy my age. Gay kids were not "out" in those days. In 1976, a kid coming out in high school would have made the evening news. There is nothing to talk about in that regard. I never had sex with a guy. I was just too straight acting. Guys never picked up on my gaydar. I was staying in the closet.

Exposed to the San Jose State University criminal justice program through the police cadet program, I enrolled in college and moved to San Jose, California. On my first day on campus, my new roommate and I happened to walk by the student union building. The new gay student union was having its first meeting. I steered away. I was terrified of being near there and curious at the same time. It was the very beginning of gay rights on campus being "the norm." Believe it or not, in 1977, there was no such thing as being "mainstream" and being gay. The only guys who went to the gay student union were obviously gay. That place to me was for lisping "fems" and "bull dykes." That wasn't me. Pass. I had a lot to learn about myself and others. The truth was that I wasn't viewing myself as "gay like that." After all, I had fucked girls many times. I was straight. Besides, this is college. I'm starting over! Of course, I was playing a stupid game on myself.

In May of 1979, my father took me to dinner for my twentieth birthday. By now, I had deluded myself into thinking that the dreaded "phase" was over. I don't know why I felt that way. The fantasies were still there. I had it under control. Really, I did. That is, until the waiter arrived at my twentieth birthday. Previously, I had never taken an interest in a grown-up guy. My interests had always been toward guys I knew, peers. Not strangers.

The waiter. He was twenty-three, blond haired with blue eyes, and he had a body to die for. He was just gorgeous. I was shocked. I couldn't take my eyes off him all night. I actually startled myself because I was so overcome by my desire for some guy I had never seen before. This had never happened before! But now, I couldn't deny it. I'm gay. It's never, ever going away. I still have the ring my father gave me that night. I can still describe the waiter.

You hear people ask, "When did you know you were gay? I don't mean when you first had a crush on another guy. I mean when, as an adult, you knew you were gay and nothing was going to change that." For me, my twentieth birthday was that moment. I had deluded myself into thinking that I would grow out of it. I was twenty. I had been smitten by a waiter. I was gay. Me of all people. Gay.

In college, I didn't date. I tried. Girls by then were picking up on a vibe or something, because girls ignored me. I tried to date, but I just wasn't getting anywhere. This wasn't going unnoticed, either. A girl who lived in the same apartment complex as me proudly described herself as a nymphomaniac. We had been friends for four years, and we had somehow ended up as roommates, sharing a two-bedroom apartment. One afternoon, she threw open the door to her bedroom, jumped back on her bed naked, spread her legs as wide as she could, and asked me if I wanted to fuck her. Although I probably would have fucked her under different circumstances, the way she delivered the offer left me stunned. It was delivered as an accusation, as a challenge. When I just stood there and mumbled an excuse, she asked the question no one had ever asked. The question wasn't asked as a friend might ask. It wasn't asked in sympathy. It wasn't asked as an olive branch. It was asked as an accusation. "Are you fucking gay?" she asked. If she had asked the question with any sort of compassion whatsoever, I might have told her the truth that day. We were actually very good friends. Instead, I was so hurt, so crushed, so devastated by the tone in which it was delivered, that I burned my one last chance to set things right. I told her what any macho straight guy would say. I told her to go fuck herself.

I nailed the closet door shut, sealed it with concrete, turned out the lights, and joined the San Francisco Police Department a few weeks later. I entered the San Francisco Police Department as part of the 151st Recruit Class in June of 1982.

The words "gay" and "homosexual" (there's that word again) were in the news all the time. The city had just recently had the White Night Riots. The riots were sparked when a former SFPD Irish Catholic kid turned disgruntled city supervisor (city councilman) named Dan White assassinated Mayor George Moscone and openly gay city supervisor and gay rights activist Harvey Milk. White was let off by the jury with a manslaughter conviction, the jury having believed the infamous "Twinkie defense," a verdict and a miscarriage of justice that stands as bad as any miscarriage of justice ever delivered. The gay community held a march that turned violent. It escalated into a full riot by thousands of gays. Police cars were overturned, set afire, and city hall was attacked. Humiliated, the cops took out revenge. The cops marched into the Castro and quite simply gay bashed everyone at the Elephant Walk Bar. The patrons of the bar weren't committing a crime; the cops were the only ones breaking the law. I have talked to and worked with cops who were there. Many were proud of what they did. The Elephant Walk was San Francisco's Stonewall. This was not at all a good time to come out.

We had one openly gay guy in my recruit class. Although he was a full-size grown man with an impressive weightlifter's body, he betrayed himself when he spoke and when we boxed in the academy. He spoke and fought like a girl. (I'm not that sort of gay.)

Following the White Night Riots and the invasion of the Elephant Walk Bar, things began to change. As part of their efforts at community outreach and to mend fences with the gay community as well as other groups, the SFPD Academy curriculum included a week of community outreach, which included a day visiting the gay community—or, as we academy recruits put it, "Gay Day."

San Francisco is a physically small city. It has a hundred neighborhoods all crammed into forty-nine square miles. One can literally walk two or three blocks and be in a completely different culture. In 1982, there were three distinct gay communities in San Francisco—the Castro, Polk Gulch, and South of Market. One was known for bath houses and S&M (South of Market or SOMA), one for boy sex and streetwalkers (Polk Gulch), and one for political activism (the Castro). This was highlighted each and every year by a show of guys in leather, feathers, chaps, and harnesses walking along with gay nuns and outlandish transvestites in the gay parade. Despite the Castro being only a few minutes from my world growing up, I had never visited it because to do so would risk being seen in the Castro. We city kids avoided it like the plague. My "Gay Day" visit to the Castro stands out in only two regards.

I remember going into a gay bar and looking up at the wall. Running on the wall was a projected film or video of a guy getting fucked from behind. Actually, a close-up of a guy getting fucked from behind, shot from behind. Two giant testicles, each projected to thirty inches across, giant pink balls swinging on the wall as music went *thump, thump,* and *thump.* Two really big, basketball-sized balls. My reaction was, and remains to this day, that you don't get people to accept you by running a video of sixty inches of scrotum fucking a guy in the ass. The Castro left me feeling like "my gay" and "their gay" were not the same. The second memory that stands out from "Gay Day" was that the cop who took us on the visit remarked, "You would do very good down here." (I'm not this kind of gay!)

One day, I went over to my dad's. I was about twenty-four years old. When my father came to the door, I told him that I had something to tell him. To this day, I don't recall what it was; it wasn't of any significance. Standing in the open door, my dad exclaimed, "You're gay!" smiling and chuckling. It was delivered as an insult, a dig, a mean remark. My dad never said anything to anyone in our family in a nice, polite way when there was a vicious, mean, and hurtful way to say it. It carried over into his humor. He was a total prick. "What? Huh? What are you talking about?" I replied. This was out of the clear blue sky. My dad had no clue that I was gay. He thought he was being funny. It stung. It once again confirmed to me that being gay wasn't the norm; it was a weakness. It meant you were less than a man.

I finished the police academy in October of 1982 as a member of the 151st Recruit Class. We had started with forty-eight classmates and finished the academy with thirty-three. By the end of field training, only twenty-seven remained, including our sole openly gay classmate. His name was Dennis. He died of AIDS a few years ago after twenty-five years as a cop, and he should be commended. I'm embarrassed today to admit that, back then, I didn't realize how historical and courageous that man was being. It was only 1982, and gay rights were not that far along, certainly not in policing. I don't recall a single person trying to be his friend, and virtually no one spoke to him.

Overall, the San Francisco Police Academy left me bored and unchallenged. I had already put myself through the San Jose Police Academy, and the curriculum there had been significantly more challenging than San Francisco's. I finished second in my class, first place going to a cop who would later become a good friend.

To me, field training was a blur. I was assigned downtown at Central

Police Station right on the edge of Chinatown. I don't think I ever left our car sector, the Tenderloin, the entire time. Central Police Station, located far away in North Beach, hadn't been in the central part of San Francisco in over one hundred years. The area is famous as the Barbary Coast from the gold rush days, and it remained that way well into the twentieth century. The Central District covers world -famous North Beach, Broadway, Fisherman's Wharf, Coit Tower, Nob Hill, Chinatown, Union Square, the financial district (where the iconic Transamerica Pyramid stands), and sadly, the Tenderloin.

The "one-car sector" of Central Station, the Tenderloin, is just a big shit hole of junkies, whores, robbers, sex freaks, drunks, and thugs. Everyone is on parole or just arrived in town with the Cuban Mariel Boatlift. The Mariel Boatlift was a mass exodus of Cubans who departed from Cuba's Mariel Harbor for the United States between April 15 and October 31, 1980. The event was precipitated by a sharp downturn in the Cuban economy, which led to internal tensions on the island and a bid by up to ten thousand Cubans to gain asylum in the Peruvian embassy.

The Cuban government subsequently announced that anyone who wanted to leave could do so, and an exodus by boat started shortly afterward. The exodus was organized by Cuban Americans with the agreement of Cuban President Fidel Castro. The exodus started having negative political implications for US President Jimmy Carter when it was discovered that a number of the exiles had been released from Cuban jails and mental health facilities.

The Mariel Boatlift was ended by mutual agreement between the two governments involved in October 1980. By that point, as many as 125,000 Cubans had made the journey to Florida. In addition, Castro had thrown many into prison for homosexual activity. After years of living in Cuban prisons, these were not smooth-bodied boys from the Castro. These were hard-core, violent parolees and prison transvestites.

The Cubans transformed the Tenderloin. We responded to a lot of Cuban homosexual fights. Drag queens high on speed. Fights with shirtless gay Cubans, covered in prison tattoos and prison scars, armed with machetes and lipstick. This didn't set a good example for the gay community or young closeted cops. (I'm not that kind of gay.)

To make matters worse, the SFPD in the 1980s was still "old school." This would all end within a decade. When I joined the SFPD, it was just emerging from policing in the 1940s and 1950s, even though it was now the 1980s. Fitting in was important. This meant drinking on the job if your FTO drank, the sergeant drank, or the lieutenant drank. This meant every night. Not a problem. You were expected to show that you were tough. Drinking gives you false courage, so it all worked out. By the third night of FTO, our meals always included wine. Our 7M (meal break) was always taken at Original Joe's on Mason Street. Original Joe's served the cops "Italian coffee," which came in a ceramic coffee pot filled with red wine. I tried not having Italian coffee with my dinner only one time and got such a look from my FTO that I never dared pass on the Italian coffee again. If my FTO had a "special beverage," I had a "special beverage."

About three weeks into the program, my FTO (nicknamed Ripper) and I were assigned to "Adam 31," the paddy wagon. The wagon's primary role is to pick up everyone's prisoners and move the station's prisoners from temporary holding down to the city prison at the Hall of Justice. A tremendous amount of time was spent dealing with drunks, either booking them at the drunk tank or by "relocating" them to some industrial area of the city and simply dragging the comatose drunks out and leaving them miles from the tourist trade. The practice finally stopped in the early 1990s when a dead body was found on the end of an old pier with the police officer's handcuffs still on the corpse. Let me assure you, downtown San Francisco was a lot cleaner back then than it is today.

That evening, Ripper and I had stopped at the Taj, an Indian restaurant in the district. We walked inside and sat down at the bar in uniform. My partner introduced me to the bartender. Ripper had obviously been there several times, and he knew what to order. As I sat wondering when my life turned into a Joseph Wambaugh novel, I watched the bartender mix us up two "pimscups," which are an Indian version of the Long Island ice tea, except it is served in a sixteen-ounce iced pewter mug. I think a pimscup must really be "bartender's choice," because it seemed like the man was pouring a little bit, and sometimes a not so little bit, of everything the bar had to offer into the chilled mugs.

Those bulletproof vests sure do get a man dehydrated! Cheers! At this point, I was fed up with being anxious and nervous about getting kicked out of FTO. The truth was that back then—and this holds true to an extent in virtually all agencies today—that during the FTO program, if they don't like you, no matter how competent you are, you are gone. They can, and still do, find ways to terminate you for "performance." To the same extent, if they like you because your dad's a cop or maybe you can play on the department football team, they find a way to keep you from being fired. Who you knew counted for a lot. For example, back during the academy, the entire emergency driving instructor cadre, fed up with woman and "others" they saw as unfit for police work, conspired to fire eight recruits in one day. The driving course had a "pass-fail" section where the officer drives at high speed toward three coned traffic lanes, left, right, and center. In today's academy, the car hits an electronic sensor, and suspended signal lights change to two reds and one green, forcing the driver to rapidly swerve into the proper lane without knocking over any cones. In 1982, there was no sensor and no lights—only the instructor sitting in the car alongside the recruit and three traffic lanes to swerve to. On cue, and at a specific designated point, the instructor would shout "Left!" "Center!" "Right!" or "Stop!" If the commands are given at the proper time, a decent driver with good reflexes and skills has just enough room to make the maneuver—but given just a moment late and the best driver in the world wasn't going to avoid the cones. One afternoon, eleven recruits went out for "pass-fail" training, and only three came back. Eight, all recruits that were bristling the academy staff because they were being perceived as being given a "minority pass," had been terminated.

Missing was one officer who was perceived by his mannerisms as being gay but wasn't open and as far as anyone knew was straight. The department was under a court-mandated consent decree to hire certain numbers of woman and minorities, and as a direct result, certain classmates were being seen as being given a "pass" when their performance was embarrassingly poor and obvious to everyone.

The driving course was unique in that there was no way to grieve any portion of the course. If the administration of the driving course was unfair or flawed, there was no way to challenge a failure. If the staff said you failed, well, then, you failed, and you were promptly dismissed. The shit hit the fan when the veteran driving instructors, sans eight minority police recruits, returned that afternoon from the Candlestick Park driving course. *Everyone* knew what had happened and that the course had been rigged to make the recruits fail. Little was done to hide that fact. The administration was angry but had no way to reverse the instructors' "failure" grade and subsequent termination of the recruits. Little effort was made to hide the actions of the instructors. The next week, the driving course was equipped with automatic lights and sensors.

(Hey. I'm a faggot. You know, one of "those." Did I mention that?)

Now, well into the middle of field training, I was getting an idea of how the game was played. Follow whatever rules your FTO follows—or in a lot of cases, doesn't follow—like drinking on duty. So when I finished my second pimscup, I opted for a third. Screw it. The bartender was just serving me when the lieutenant walked in. "You going to the 49ers game this weekend, Rip?" asked the lieutenant to my FTO while simultaneously sitting down at the bar stool next to me. I was frozen still, staring at the pimscup, wondering when the lieutenant was going to chew me out and fire me for drinking. I needn't have bothered. My concern over my frosty mug evaporated with the lieutenant smiled and warned me to not "get out of control" with those pimcups. The lieutenant then ordered one for himself.

I had finished my third pimscup when the restaurant maître d' came into the bar informing us of an unruly drunk trying to barge into the restaurant. My FTO indicated that I should go solve the problem. The lieutenant and my FTO swiveled their bar stools around to watch as they sipped from the chilled pewter mugs. The unruly man was a drunken tourist, a mainstay of policing in San Francisco. As I stood to perform my official duties, I discovered that California clearly had fallen into the Pacific Ocean during the last sixty minutes, because the entire world was rocking and spinning. Taking a deep breath, I mumbled and slurred, "I got it, Louie," and sauntered over to eject the drunk. The drunk wanted no part of leaving and tried to push past me to get into the bar. Already ill-tempered and ill-mannered after months of trying to fit in, I was just not in the mood to have some drunk make me look timid or foolish, no matter how drunk I was. I slammed him into a wall, applying everything I had into a rear wrist lock, and I walked him out the door, up the stairs to the street, and slammed him into the back of the paddy wagon with a metallic and hollow *wham*! Just for dramatic effect, I threw in a few "motherfuckers" and "assholes" at the drunk just like I had read about in *The New Centurions*, because that book seemed more like the SFPD code of conduct than the department general orders. In the meantime, my FTO and the lieutenant had trailed behind me discussing the upcoming football schedule and who had season tickets. They had warned us in the academy not to expect your FTO to help you if you got in trouble. If someone gave you a hard time, short of a guy going for your gun or a gun of his own, the expectation was that the recruit should display, demonstrate, and give his or her 100 percent commitment to a fight. There was no expectation that you could take on everyone and bring them down, only that you were willing to give it you all, be that 125 or 225 pounds. Penis or clitoris. 100 percent.

I had passed my test. I was going to finish FTO. I was going to become a probationary police officer. In the meantime, the gay sex thing was well under control. Maybe it really was a phase? I loved my job and threw myself into it. When I finished the field training program at Central Station, I was sent to Potrero (now Bayview) Station. Located in San Francisco's decaying industrial portion, it is nothing but miles of public housing, unemployment, and poverty. It was and remains today the most dangerous and violent part of San Francisco. Housed at Twentieth and Third Streets, the station house was picked right off of the set of *Barney Miller*. A NYPD-style precinct house sitting in San Francisco, built at the turn of the century, was going to be my home for the next eight years.

At Bayview Station, I found out what being a street cop was all about. Every night, there was a shooting, a chase, a stabbing, a murder, and all the cops tried to outdo the other in making felony arrests. We never had enough backup, and we always made do with balls and bravado. Prisoners frequently got "lumped" at the station booking counter, and drinking on duty was still a problem. The bar next door served the entire day watch cocktails to officers in uniform. The cops were in there all day long. A dead body once rotted in a car parked in the red zone between the bar and the front door of the station. It was only a five-foot walk from the station to the bar, and you had to walk right past this illegally parked car. For three days, the body sat in the front seat of the car, red zone and all, as shift after shift of cops walked past to get "pops" at the bar. A citizen finally complained about the smell.

It seems so unbelievable looking back. Back then, the job was real rough-and-tumble, and the Potrero was a very macho place to work. The station abutted against rows of shipyard and steelworker bars, the same bars that the dockworkers, shipbuilders, and sailors of WWII drank at not many years before. And although I saw some cops unfit for duty, I never saw one take a bribe or steal something, and I never saw anyone get "lumped" who didn't deserve it.

I was working in an environment, particularly in public housing, where the cops were and still are an occupying force. At every arrest, you ran the risk of a mob lynching your prisoner. More often than not, you had rocks and bottles tossed at you. Traffic stops at the wrong intersection would guarantee sniper fire. There were locations where you never did a traffic stop. At night, you would get shot at from the shadows. It was a very violent environment, and as a cop, you had to prove yourself. Suspects rarely complied with being handcuffed and would never, ever do so in a crowd. To try to arrest a suspect in a crowd bordered on foolhardy. A patrolman might as well as broadcast "Officer needs help," the second he reached for the handcuff case.

Everybody always ran from us. Police cars left unattended had tires slashed, windows broken, and worse.

One evening while serving a search warrant in the Potrero Hill housing projects, we left the five radio cars in front of the place. Halfway through the search warrant, an officer called for help with "shots fired" a mile away. We ran out to the cars, and I cranked up the engine of my car. I noticed something strange. A blue glow was coming out from between the cracks of the hood of my police car. Revving the engine, I noticed that my partner wasn't jumping in the car. In fact, none of the cops were doing anything. "Come on, you guys! Shots fired! Come on!"

"We aren't going anywhere, Pete. Look." I got out of the car. All the tires were slashed. The blue glow I had seen was the last of the lighter fluid burning off from under the hood where they tried to torch the car. All the other police cars had shattered windows and slashed tires. Each and every car.

The Potrero had places like the Waterloo Lounge and Third and Gilman, which was a black parolee bar sitting right in the main patrol corridor, Third Street. Driving by meant that you had to roll up the windows so that the bottles might shatter on the car window instead of hitting you in the head. If you could identify who threw the bottle, or in many cases just who threw a verbal "Fuck you," you were expected to jump out of the car and arrest the guy. No backup. Jump out of the car and challenge the crowd. Find the guy, knock him down, and hook him up. My partner was once in such a rage to grab a guy who yelled "Fuck the police" that he actually tore off the inside door handle in the radio car.

The Geneva Towers. They were two identical buildings—forty stories of public housing. Our police radios didn't work inside at all. The building security was on the take. You couldn't ever stand or park in front because you would get hit by a car jack, shopping cart, bottles, and trash falling twenty stories onto you. Even an orange falling that far makes quite a *whack* when it hits, as does a shopping cart on the window of my brand-new radio car with fifteen miles on it. The elevators in the building took twenty minutes to go up or down. It took forever for your backup to get to you. A friend of mine responded at 4:00 a.m. to a domestic dispute involving a knife at the Towers. Upon entering the apartment, the suspect took his wife hostage at knifepoint and then immediately began stabbing her with a nine-inch carving knife. The officer couldn't get a shot with his pistol, and his partner had the police shotgun. The first officer jumped in and began to fight for the knife, only to get stabbed repeatedly through his vest. The worst was yet to come. His partner jammed the barrel of the twelve-gauge shotgun against the suspect's ribs and pulled the trigger, killing him instantly. The cop had failed to notice that the muzzle of the Remington was pressed against his fellow officer's forearm. The officer, an accomplished pianist, had his arm 90 percent severed. The place was a hellhole. The building elevator interiors were literally riddled with bullet holes. It took a lot of guts for a young white cop to walk by himself into this place armed only a .38 revolver. (A guy who does this can't be gay!)

The mid-1980s brought crack cocaine, and a place that was violent already got many times worse. To this day, these communities have never been the same. At about this time, I learned what it meant to be gay at a busy "working station." One afternoon, I heard someone talking about a guy I had worked around for a few years. JD was all cop. All tough guy. He had been married and had kids. One of my co-workers informed me that JD was gay. I was really surprised, not only because he didn't fit the stereotype of a gay guy, but because no one seemed to care or notice that JD was gay. It wasn't even gossip. Why? It was because JD did his job. He showed courage, integrity, toughness, dedication, and professionalism.

I worked up the courage to ask him about being married and being gay. I was so impressed by the guy. There really wasn't much to discuss, he said. He said that he was gay. He said that he always had been gay. He got married and had wonderful kids. He eventually discovered that he couldn't hide from who he was, and this was his only shot at life. So he came out to San Francisco and joined the SFPD and came out of the closet. As far as what JD had to say about police work and being gay? "Just do your job. That's all these guys care about." JD would soon die of AIDS. Many of the potential gay male role models would go with him, a plague that to this day leaves its mark on the police department. Despite JD's words, at twenty-five, I was devoted to staying in the closet. It would take me another fifteen years before I could believe JD's words. "Just do your job."

The violence of the Potrero District had another significant impact on my life. I wanted a bigger gun. In the mid-1980s, SFPD cops carried .357 Magnum revolvers, but the department downgraded us to a .38 round, and in fact, to a custom-made .38 round the manufacturer called the Plus-P-Plus. It was a total failure, with suspects commonly absorbing six solid, close-range hits and not going down. The revolvers were little more than popguns. The truth of the matter was that the new breed of female and small male cops couldn't fire a .357 magnum. They had dumbed down a good man stopper, the .357 magnum, to accommodate the new recruits.

Potrero Station. 1983. A veteran female officer made the mistake of taking on King Kong, the robbery suspect. She was alone in a crowd in front of the Waterloo Lounge. No one had ever questioned this officer's ability to do her job. She was competent, courageous, and a capable cop.

She made a terrible error in judgment.

No one told King Kong, six foot six and 280 pounds of San Quentin muscle, that she was a good cop. It didn't matter to him. On the streets, your past deeds mean nothing. No sooner had the officer spotted the armed robbery suspect and challenged him then he swung around and landed a roundhouse punch square in her face. He knocked her to the ground and on her back. The suspect began punching her some more, beating her in the face, eventually ripping the six-inch .357 magnum from her holster and beating her across the face with it. Then he stood up and took aim at her head, preparing to finish the job. Many a cop had been gunned down in this neighborhood. The suspect's companion yelled, "No, man! Don't do it! Don't do it!" Fortunately for the lady cop, the suspect decided that he wasn't going to be a cop killer that day, at least not in front of seventy-five witnesses. He jumped into a getaway car and fled.

Within a few minutes, an informant called the station and supplied the description and address of the wanted vehicle, and a few minutes into a stakeout, we had one suspect in custody. The primary assailant and the officer's gun were still outstanding. We wanted him. We wanted that gun.

That night, I was working with a veteran black cop. The man was as dark as coal, tough as iron, and he wasn't scared of a soul. He was a mean bastard. He was so mean and tough that the people in the neighborhood respected him to where he didn't even need to wear a bulletproof vest. No one had the guts to shoot at him. I was twenty-three years old. Worse, I looked fourteen. I had blond hair and blue eyes. I was a kid. I was brand-new to the station. I had heard horror stories about police brutality. I had studied ethics in law enforcement. I knew what the "right thing to do" was. I had listened to college professors. I listened at the academy. I had a degree in criminal justice from San Jose State University. I was the modern faux-liberal policeman. That was all going to be put to the test.

We transported the handcuffed suspect back to the station house as every cop in the city started looking for the suspect, hoping to get the officer's revolver back. Without a word being said, officers who had been changing into civvies to go home went back in uniform, grabbed any black-and-white that ran, and hit the streets. It didn't hurt that the suspect would likely be armed and could be shot virtually on sight, something everyone at the station wanted to personally accommodate.

This was a very dangerous neighborhood. Cops had been routinely targeted for assassination over the last decade. Many radicals from the Black Liberation Army and the Black Panthers called this place home. You could start a riot out here with one misstep. When we arrived in the station parking lot with the prisoner, it was late—almost midnight. The station had an apartment building next to it—one wall of windows overlooking the police lot. The windows were all dark. Otherwise, no one could see us.

I unlocked the back door to the station in preparation for bringing the suspect into the holding area. The suspect, who was in the caged radio car, was being helped out by my partner. The next sixty seconds were a nightmare.

"Get on your fucking knees! Get *down* on your *motherfucking* knees!" I turned. I couldn't believe what I was seeing. This can't be happening. My partner had his pistol out by his side. The suspect, still handcuffed, was standing right in front of him. "Get on your fucking knees right now!" my partner barked again. The suspect was terrified. He slunk to his knees, and whatever composure he might have had evaporated. I didn't know what was going on, but the suspect did, and he was about to shit his pants. I had been a cop for six months. The suspect, on his knees, was pleading and crying, "Please, no man! Please, no man! No man!" He kept chanting that over and over. Almost three decades later, I can still see his face and feel the moment. My partner had only one thing to say before he rudely shoved his revolver in the suspect's mouth. "I'm going to count to three, and you are going to tell me the motherfucker's name and where that gun is, or I'm going to blow your motherfucking brains out! *One!*" The suspect was crying and trying to plead, but it was kind of hard to do with the pistol's front sight jammed in the back of his throat.

"*Two!*" I heard the *click* and watched my partner pull back the hammer on his revolver. His finger was resting on the trigger. Two and one half pounds of spring tension were keeping this man alive. For now.

My partner slid just enough of the gun out of the man's mouth to find out if he was ready to talk.

This has to be a dream! We don't put black men on their knees and execute them! This isn't the south of the 1950s! *This isn't happening! You can't do this!* my mind screamed. I thought of pulling my gun. I began to slowly move my hand toward my holster. I vividly remember wondering if I was actually going to have shoot my partner.

I'd like to tell you that I did something noble or heroic. I remember looking up at the apartment windows. The windows were black, but that didn't mean someone wasn't watching. I was wondering who was going to see this and how it is going to make the Watts Riots look tame. My hand was moving too slow, probably on purpose, because even at that moment, I knew that I didn't have the balls to do it. I don't think my partner was going to back down, because he wasn't thinking of the consequences. Before the number three and a gunshot, the suspect began blabbering and crying, and he quickly told us who to look for. Within an hour, the wanted suspect and the officer's gun were back in the station. (This station probably isn't the place to bring up the gay thing.)

I loved patrol. I was seeing more action here at Potrero with its tons of public housing than one would ever wish to see. At twenty-four, I was abating family fights and going to family stabbings and drug shootings. I was getting in pursuits of stolen cars. Everyone was assumed to be armed. I once took a .30-30 Winchester Model 94 off a guy on a shots fired call. Wearing nothing but jeans and a T-shirt, the man appeared unarmed. The witnesses insisted that the man still had the weapon. They were right. He had removed the shoulder stock and stuck the loaded rifle down his leg. I clearly needed something bigger than a .38 revolver. The only big guns in the SFPD belonged to the specialist team guys. They had AR-15s and shotguns. I wanted an AR-15 assault rifle. Screw this popgun bullshit.

In 1983, I tried out for and was selected as a patrolman on the specialist team. Over the next few years, I advanced to a position on the training staff, and by 1988 was running the tactical training for the entire specialist team. I became an FBI-trained and certified sniper. A firearms instructor. A tactical firearms instructor. A survival shooting instructor. A crowd control instructor.

I also discovered that I was becoming a "go-to" guy by patrol sergeants, tactical members, and commanding officers. I was running many successful SWAT operations as a tactical team member and fell into a natural—at least for me—position of leadership. Bosses asked me for advice and listened to what I had to say.

The 1980s was also a period of a lot of demonstrations. We hosted the 1984 Democratic National Convention, the International Conference on AIDS, and dozens and dozens of violent street protests against everything under the sun. The specialist team, the tactical company, and, at that time, the MUNI (Transit) platoon were the core of SFPD crowd and riot control, and we made literally thousands of arrests at protests. We proudly hit more hippies and liberals than, well, hell, more than anyone! Within a couple of years, my radio car partner, a big bruiser of an Irishman, introduced me to the woman I would marry, Norma. Norma and I hit it off instantly. She had left home at twenty with a round-trip ticket to San Francisco, and—like so many twenty-year-olds before her—she decided to cash out the rest of her ticket and stay in San Francisco. Norma and I matched instantly. And just like that, I wasn't gay.

Our relationship was natural. Before I knew it, I was stopping off at Norma's on my way home from work and just never, ever got to my apartment in the Sunset District. We'd make love all night in a little city flat on Broderick Street with its century-old bathtub with its big lion feet.

It was a great time. The best way to understand why I liked Norma is to tell you a story that happened in 1986. Norma's place on Broderick Street was a half a block from public housing. There is a liquor store on the corner where drunks and thugs hang out and drink forty ouncers. Norma got off the bus at the corner at about three in the afternoon when some little housing thug snatched her purse. Her Louis Vuitton purse. Wrong! Norma chased the little robber through public housing, cornered him, and made the kid give it back. This was my type of woman!

When I first met Norma, she was suffering from what was then diagnosed as epilepsy. She had occasional petit mal seizures where she would completely disconnect for a few minutes and then come back. She wouldn't fall to the ground and fully seize; she would just sort of "brain seize." It prevented her from driving, of course, but that is easily overcome in San Francisco with wide-reaching and convenient public transit. Norma had previously worked at a big Wall Street and now defunct investment and brokerage house as a stenographer. Sitting in on high-level board meetings, she would have no trouble keeping up while taking high-end dictation and then later typing up the work. Eventually, the epilepsy became a problem at work, and she was let go, but she quickly found other work. I didn't see the epilepsy as a big issue for Norma and me. I had now seen that life wasn't a storybook for many of us. You have to take the good with the bad. People get sick. That's not a reason to abandon them. That is simply such a core part of my belief system. I don't want fair-weather friends that are here only in good times. True friends are friends in bad times, too. This, to me, is a true judge of character in a person.

By 1987, Norma and I had moved in together and were engaged. It all flowed so naturally. I had simply found "my grove" with this woman. I had a true friend and partner. I didn't really think about gay too much. I figured that dragon had been slain. Months before the wedding, Norma's seizures became more frequent and severe and had grown into grand mal seizures. These were terrifying things, with all the contortions and shaking and foaming at the mouth. It's horrible to see someone you love have these seizures. Norma and I bonded even closer, because I was now there for her in another way. I was becoming a caregiver for her. I didn't mind. Of course I would have preferred Norma to be in perfect health, but all of this simply wasn't a huge relationship issue for us. She was having some problems, and I was going to be there for her.

Norma's medical bills were all paid by her out of pocket, frequently on 20 percent interest rate credit cards because that's the only way she could keep up with her uninsured health costs. Once Norma and I became engaged, we had decided to immediately get her onto my insurance and to get a full, fresh diagnosis of her seizure disorder. My father, a highly skilled and much respected vascular surgeon, was having misgivings about the epilepsy diagnosis, as was I. Although Norma had had head CTs before, her diagnosis of psychomotor epilepsy was looking suspicious.

Buried in a five-year-old head CT lab report was a passing reference to a mass that needed further enhancing and investigating. For some reason, the report about the mass was never passed on. We wouldn't discover that medical report for four more years. We would feel the ramifications within a few weeks, and it would last forever.

I had hated every minute of all the planning for the wedding. It seemed endless. I was a Jewish doctor's son. What can I say? But I can tell you this. I was truly happy and joyful when I watched Norma walk down that isle. It was then, and is even today, the happiest day of my life. It really was. That day I had promised her my love and devotion, in sickness and in health, until death do us part. That's why it all hurts all so much. Even today. Especially today.

The second day of our honeymoon, the wheels came off. We had rested up from a long flight that had departed at 6:00 a.m. They lost our luggage. We were hot and tired and didn't like the locals who seemed to think being rude was a hobby. Norma and I had slept pretty much through the first evening on Maui, having arrived very late in the afternoon. This had been our first night of true rest in several days. The week had started with the final hectic preparations for the wedding, the rehearsal, the rehearsal dinner, the wedding, the reception, and the travel. But now it's a fresh morning. It's a fresh day in a beautiful room in Hawaii. Finally, we could stop and relax and be together as husband and wife. What's straighter than a honeymoon?

Then the seizures started. The first one came and went, but then she had another, and later another. It seemed that as soon as she had recovered from one, she suffered another. Norma had them all week, and they were terrible ones that lasted for several minutes and left her exhausted for the rest of the day. It was heartbreaking. This was supposed to be such a special time for her. I don't remember a normal day in my life after that first morning in Maui. Because of the seizures coming so soon on the heels of the wedding day, many of her memories of the ceremony were being erased. Norma and I wouldn't be on a vacation again for many, many years. As soon as we returned from our honeymoon, we got Norma to Stanford University. They have the best doctors in the world who deal with brain disorders (or so they say).

They batted fifty-fifty that day. They were right in one regard. They discovered that Norma didn't have epilepsy; she had an astrocytoma in her brain. A brain tumor. They were wrong in the other regard. They told us that it was inoperable. Fatal and terminal. Go home. Norma and I sat at home. We just sat. I mean, what the fuck can you say? Our lives together had just begun, and the outlook looked grim.

My father asked around and discovered that a surgeon named Charlie Wilson at the University of California Medical Center San Francisco was doing stuff no one else did. Ironically, we lived just a few blocks from UCSF. One day, a bunch of buildings mean nothing to you, and the next day, those buildings are the center of your life. So on a September morning, Norma and I smoked our last cigarette together. We stood out in front of the hospital on Parnassus Street. We talked one last time. I didn't know it at that time, but I would never talk to Norma, the woman I married, again. Not that Norma. The risk of death in the surgery was high. The risk of brain injury was high. The doctors, of course, had given us all the warnings one gets before one has surgery. This can happen. That can happen. Deafness. Blindness. Loss of memory. Paralysis. Loss of brain function. The surgeon, Charley Wilson, said he was confident that if he could remove the tumor cleanly, the outcome would be good. We ignored the "if" as much as we could. The surgery was dangerous and destructive. We had no choice. Go home and have seizures until you die, or have the surgery and risk brain damage. You can't believe that this is happening, so you grasp onto one thought. It will turn out okay.

So we smoked a last cigarette. We went upstairs to the surgery ward. They shaved her head. It was horrible beyond words. Norma was always so proud of her beautiful hair. She was crying as they shaved her bald. Two months later, we were in another therapy session for Norma. She was learning how to read and write again. She was wearing a scarf. It covered the fact that she lost all of her hair to radiation. It hid the part of her head where they put back the bone plate, and it covered the scar.

We'd gone to a place on Powell Street a few weeks before to buy a woman's wig. It was upstairs off the street. Supposedly, it was the place to buy the best wigs in town. Norma tried on a few. The saleslady had just approached when Norma just couldn't take it anymore. She simply fell apart. This obviously wasn't the first time the saleslady had seen a young pretty bald woman with cancer break down in tears. This wasn't the first time a woman had finally been crushed by the unfairness of it all. I looked at the saleslady. She knew. Without any of us saying a word, Norma and I walked out the door.

In the fantasy movie of your life, the doctor walks down the hallway and tells you the good news. Or, if it's bad news, they take you to a clean, quiet place and gently break the news. Life isn't a movie. We had been warned that Dr. Wilson's surgical skills were the best that there were but that his bedside manner wasn't of the same caliber. He is legendary on both counts. Everyone was right.

Six hours after the surgery began, Norma's dad and I walked out of the cafeteria hallway just as Dr. Wilson approached. We had been playing poker for pennies in the cafeteria as we waited to hear how the surgery went. Norma's father Sam and I approached the doctor, him still in his green scrubs and little booties. There wasn't going to be a private little room, just a hallway outside a cafeteria. "Hi. She's fine. She's in recovery. She did well. We wanted to get most of it if it was encapsulated. It wasn't. It was more sticky and invasive. We got 60 percent of it. We couldn't get it all. It would have damaged too much more. She will need radiation. The survival rate is 40 percent in five years. See me in my office when she is discharged."

Um, excuse me. This isn't supposed to be happening—40 percent alive in five years is 60 percent *dead*! In the end, the list of long-term brain damage from the Norma's brain surgery sounds much like the list of things we were warned about, but in much finer detail. Norma did indeed suffer a loss of brain function, as the doctors called it presurgery. In Norma's case, this meant complete and total loss of short-term memory. She now forgets what you say almost as fast as you tell it to her and as fast as she hears it. She can't remember anything she reads. She can't learn anything new and has difficulty remembering the old.

Aphasia. Ever have a word on the tip of your tongue? That's aphasia. That happens to Norma with virtually each and every sentence like a stutter of the brain. If she gets stuck, she will simply use any word or words—even if they mean the opposite or don't relate at all—in place of the word that's stuck on the tip of her tongue. It's maddening and frustrating for both her and the listener. Her lack of short-term memory makes learning new tasks impossible. She repeats everything dozens of times. Give Norma a field sobriety test and she would fail it one hundred times out of one hundred. Her sense of balance was ruined, and this deficit, as these things are medically known, would later make outdoor activities for us impossible. Her libido disappeared. She told me one day when I was in my midthirties that if she never had sex again in her life, that that would be just fine with her.

More than anything, it was the loss of Norma as an intellectual friend that made things come apart. Gay or straight, Norma's loss of intellect might have ruined our marriage. I found that even the simplest conversations with Norma had become maddening and frustrating riddles, with Norma trying so hard to express her thoughts but being unable to communicate them. I grew angry and frustrated as conversations became games of "yes" and "no" as I would vainly try to decipher the meaning of the conversation. What would be answered as a *yes* would moments later be answered with a *no*, *yesterday* would become *today*, and *it* would become *they*. Because Norma had suffered so much short-term memory loss, she compensates by telling someone the same things over and over and over. The worst part is that each and every time she tells a story or event, it is generally in contradiction of the last telling of a story she gave.

It's not her fault. There's no one to be mad at. I found myself getting angry at Norma more and more and loathing myself for not being more patient. Norma was unhappy and depressed. We were both unhappy. I thought I could deal with it. Joe cop. Specialist Pete.

We spent years dealing with Norma's rehabilitation. Her brain function was as good as it was going to get. Now, after years of doctors and rehabilitation, we were spending years in marriage counseling trying to cope with Norma's brain injury, but it was now no longer a marriage as it was me trying hard to keep my promise of "for better or for worse, in sickness and in health." We both wanted our marriage to work. Norma had gotten a raw deal, and we both wanted things back like they used to be before "the tumor," which is our phrase for the times before. I had no one to talk to. Our sex life was over. I was lonely and depressed.

After my mom committed suicide, my father had a long-term relationship with a woman, Angela, who he would eventually marry, but with more drama along the way than is worth mentioning. I liked Angela. Angela been had first been married to a man named Marshall, and they had two children together. Marshall was a wonderful guy and was a part of all of our family gatherings. He was a real joy of a human being. There are people on the good end of the bell curve, way over to the "good guy" side. That was where Marsh lived. He was also a wonderful dad to his kids. And he was gay. Angela and he had divorced, and he had come out. Marshall had suffered a nervous breakdown and ended up in the hospital. He crawled out of the closet, crawled out of depression, and rebuilt himself. In short order, he got back to being a good, hardworking, stable man, a good father to his children, and an ex-husband to Angela. I was amazed and intrigued.

One day at a gathering at my dad's home, Marsh and I sat together. We turned to the subject of him being gay. He told me his coming-out story. For fifteen minutes, he told me the story of his (my) life. I was mesmerized. He finished the story. They say that 90 percent of human communication is nonverbal. I didn't say a word. I don't think he needed the other 10 percent. I know an olive branch when I see one.

At just that moment and before I could say anything, a woman walked over and started talking to us. And with that, the little bubble— the moment—went *pop*. AIDS got Marsh a few months later. I never got to say, "Thanks, Marsh, for that olive branch." I should have taken it.

Reading this book for some advice, kids? Here's one for you. When someone reaches out to you, reach back. That might be your only chance.

In 1990, I was promoted to sergeant. If you want me to describe the perfect police job, it is a patrol sergeant. It's all the fun, but none of the paperwork. In June of 1990, I was assigned to Southern Police Station, which covers the downtown area of San Francisco south of Market Street. I had been at Southern Station one year when, in April 1991, a new task force was being established to (add sarcasm here) clean up the Tenderloin District, the same place where I had been a rookie patrolman out of Central Station. The Tenderloin is smack dab in the middle of San Francisco. It is like a butt hole in the middle of an otherwise beautiful area. Its name derives from the fact that the beat cop in the Tenderloin "got the best cut" back in the Barbary Coast days. Those days are over.

The Tenderloin is like Times Square before Mayor Giuliani. It is an overdone Hollywood movie set of junkies, prostitutes, drug dealers, con artists, meth heads, crack monsters, the mentally deranged, muggers, whores, gangbangers, Russian mafia, heroin addicts, Vietnamese mafia, Chinese gangsters, sex registrants, and all of them, of course, preying on the elderly, sick, young, and vulnerable. It is the most densely populated area of parolees west of the Mississippi. Everyone—and I mean literally everyone—who is out on the street after dark is on probation, parole, actively wanted, here illegally, a cop, or a cab driver.

The City of San Francisco doesn't have one police department; it has ten, one for each "station" or precinct. Each is as individual to the other as are the various neighborhoods of this fractured city. They all have completely different flavors from station to station, and from shift to shift. Some stations have reputations as having the best cops, the worst cops, the laziest cops, the most pussy, the best or worst bosses, the best restaurants, the most overtime, the most freebies, the best bars, and such nonsense. The "most action" is so far down the list of attributes that it doesn't even garner consideration except from about 10 percent of the cops. Not everyone fits everywhere. I don't fit at lazy or slow places.

When I started my first patrol assignment as a sergeant at Southern Station, I had come from eight years of public housing, narcotics work, and lots of SWAT time. I loved the adrenaline, and even today I still don't understand why anyone would become a cop and not want to "go play." Chase a bad guy. Make a top-notch arrest. This night shift, I was supervising the "nice guys, but lazy, but the district has good freebies cops." These cops assigned here hadn't been asked to perform at a very high level in many, many years. As one lady officer put it to me when I asked why she was never at the scene of a hot call, she replied, "Hey, Sarge, I got two kids at home. If you think I'm going to come here and get fucking hurt, you're out of your fucking mind." Seeing as she was fucking the watch commander, I figured she was a lost cause. The Tenderloin looked good to me. Fuck these assholes. I volunteered to help clean up the Tenderloin.

The Tenderloin Task Force, April Fools' Day, 1991. This police district covers such a ridiculously small area that a New York or Chicago cop would laugh in our faces if they saw that we couldn't clean it up. We could have cleaned it up, but they threw roadblocks in our way every chance they had. In five months, the sixty officers of the Tenderloin Task Force brought in 5,000 arrests. We brought in so many that we changed the violation policy of state parole. We now needed fresh felonies to violate parole. We overcrowded the jail. They started releasing them as fast as we put them in.

Drug dealing was so prevalent that a uniform beat cop bought crack *in uniform* from a dealer *next to the station*. The man was so intent on the sale that he never looked up enough to see that the cop was in uniform. The judge dismissed the case in typical San Francisco fashion, not believing that anyone could be that stupid. In our first year, it seemed that half of the officers were involved in an "officer-involved" shooting, a trend that would continue. We had so many foot chases, car chases, fights, shootings, stabbings, and gun cases that it was cop heaven. In one evening alone, we had six stabbings. The men and women became like family and bonded very closely while working out of the historic old Hibernia Bank Building at 1 Jones Street. The building is a massive stone-walled bank building that housed the police department after the fire and quake of 1906. The bank remained a bank for nearly a century—until after the 1989 Loma Prieta quake when the place was deemed unsafe and not seismically sound. Of course, they put our office in the basement of the bank so when the big quake hits, they could save the cost of burying us.

At the Tenderloin Task Force, I made a good reputation for myself as a reliable patrol sergeant, as the guy you wanted on scene for a dangerous situation. Many nights I was the acting platoon commander, sometimes for weeks at a time. Unfortunately, all the arrests and hard work in the Tenderloin hadn't done a damned thing. By then, San Francisco's liberal DAs were well into the catch-and-release method of law enforcement. Criminals were being released as quickly as we booked them.

I had also begun publishing my photography. I had been heavily involved in black-and-white photography since I was eighteen, and I had begun to take photographs while assigned to the Tenderloin Task Force. The department's public affairs unit started using my photographs, as did our union, the San Francisco Police Officers Association. For a year, in the union's monthly newspaper, I published a series of photo essays entitled "Out on Patrol." (Excuse the suddenly revealed pun). By the end of the decade, the department was displaying one hundred of my framed black-and-white photographs on the walls of the Hall of Justice. In a fortunate turn of events, these photos were seen by a book publisher back east. As a result of this exposure, my photographs were published in a book by Turner Publishing called *Blue in Black and White*. Soon I was doing book signings and even a television interview. My book appeared in area bookstores and remains available at major booksellers as well as online. Although I was never going to get rich off my book, I did appreciate how fortunate I was to get published. I was becoming known in the department, and I felt like it was all a lie.

I was also spending huge amounts of time as the executive officer of the specialist team and coordinating the training for the sixty-officer unit. We were modernizing the team in response to a deadly mass shooting that had taken place in 1993. Over the next few years, I became the face of much of the tactical instruction within the SFPD. I trained everyone from recruits to chiefs. I was on a first-name basis with virtually everyone in the department. By establishing myself in the department and by establishing a solid reputation, I had unwittingly painted myself into a corner. Just like you. This was my career. I'm not trying to impress the reader or make myself out to be some super cop. I'm not. This book is about coming out, not war stories. At some point in my life as a cop, I intertwined my accomplishments with my sexuality, as if revealing the truth would make the accomplishments disappear or be diminished.

You—like me—have many accomplishments, too. You—like me—are proud of your reputation. I have a ton of medals and commendations. Some are overblown. Some of the best work I ever did went without a medal or recognition. Who cares? If you stay available and active out on the streets and you work hard, shit is going to find you. Then you will have action. You will do this, and you will do that. You will get awards and medals. They are not a measure of anything in my mind except as a gauge of how much time a guy spends actually working in a busy district.

I have kicked down a lot of doors. I have almost been shot twice. I came close to having my finger bitten off by a wife beater. I broke my thumb being stupid enough to block a guy swinging an axe handle at some other guy who probably deserved it. I broke my other thumb, but I forget how. I have given mouth-to-mouth back when we did such a thing and CPR to many, but never, ever with success. I have arrested thousands of felons. I have been at hundreds of demonstrations, frequently in charge of a platoon. I have been punched, spit on, and kicked. I have had guns and knives pulled on me. I have done some big investigations and made some nice arrests. I have run tactical operations by the dozens and trained hundreds of officers. I have been an FTO sergeant. I have run hundreds of crime scenes and murder scenes and shooting scenes. I have been in a hundred foot pursuits. I have been involved in and managed officer-involved shootings, jumpers, mass murders. Resisters? How many resisters? How many "insane people"?

I was once asked on the witness stand by a public defender how many domestic family fight calls I had been to. When I told him thousands, he smirked aloud in court. He actually laughed aloud. He asked me how I had come to such a figure. He was incredulous. I told him that my partner and I went to about four "DV" calls a night. We worked five days a week. Four times five equals twenty. Fifty workweeks a year comes out to one thousand family fights per year. At that time, I had been in six years. Six thousand "DV" calls. Stay on the streets ten, twenty, thirty years. Do the math. Stay out and play and you do a damn lot of police work. All that work. All that time. I didn't want that to be tarnished. Being gay would tarnish it, or at least that was my thinking at that time.

When it comes to airplanes, I'm a little kid. Had it not been for the uncorrected vision restrictions of the day, I would most certainly have become an airline pilot. I had actually spent time flying "sailplanes," which everyone else knows as "gliders." There was a glider port at the Nut Tree in Vacaville, California, and I had spent a summer flying and eventually flew solo in the engineless aircraft, soaring the California thermals up to ten thousand feet.

It's 1996. We are at a party somewhere in the suburbs. The host is a jumbo jet pilot. He invited me to look at a new flight simulator program on his home computer—Microsoft Flight Simulator. Up until then, I had seen the nerds at work with their computers. It was mid-1990s, and computers were just showing up in everyday life, but I didn't see what a computer could possibly bring me. You can run spreadsheets. What's a spreadsheet? Who gives a fuck? You can send e-mail? Pass. However, tell me that I can simulate flying a jumbo jet into SFO at night in a hailstorm low on fuel? No shit? Cool! It's just like the real thing? Really? Great! (Penis says: I heard about computers. Porn.) I asked the host, "Just how real is this Microsoft flight program thing compared to really flying?" The host told me that it was exactly like the real deal. Fly a glider into Nut Tree Airport. Choose your aircraft. Got an ASK-21 glider? Sure do. Take off to the south? Want some crosswind? Here you go. Release the tow cable at five thousand feet. Look on the screen. This program is just like flying the real deal! Let me try the F-16! (Penis says: I heard about computers. Porn.) The little boy in me, along with the little head, went off and bought a computer the next day. Let the genie out. Oh, Mr. Penis, what have we done?

It's 1997. I have been online long enough now to accept, to myself, the obvious. I have not looked at a naked girl online in the year since I bought the computer. I'm a gay man. I'm thirty-eight, and I'm gay. That summer, Norma and took a vacation to Mexico. I am miserable, trying to come to grips with an unhappy marriage, guilt over Norma's illness and brain injury, and disappointed in myself for how frustrated I get with her. I'm guilt ridden over my sexuality and all the lies I seem to be creating. Wandering the beach in Mexico one afternoon, one of the jet ski rental guys tried to drum up some business. "Señor. How are you? What brings you to Mexico?"

It's my birthday, I tell him. It's my thirty-eighth birthday. He begins to laugh and replies something to me in Spanish. "What's so funny?" I ask.

"In Mexico, señor, it is at thirty-eight that a man decides. It's an old joke in Mexico, señor. That at thirty-eight, it is when a man decides he no longer likes the girls, señor. He likes the boys." He was right. I was thirty-eight. I like guys. Within months, I would take the steps that brought me to today.

The Internet has changed this planet like no other single device. It changed mine. It opened a portal to a world where there were millions of men like me. "Normal" guys, married guys. Gay married guys. Gay cops. Gay soldiers and doctors. Gay lawyers. Blue collar. White collar. Guys just like me. Everywhere. I wasn't the only guy in the world married and gay. I could talk. Chat. Vent. Porno, sure, but porn has always been around. Suddenly, here was a way I could be honest with myself and with others, but in a way that I could control. I could be anyone I wanted to be. I could find a path out of this horrible situation.

I took a path. That path got me to the place I am today. It is probably not unlike the destination I would have arrived at had I taken the right path as a young man. As far as I can tell, the destination would have been the same: the place where I am today. The path was wrong. It was very, very wrong. I have very little advice to give you guys out there, but I can say this as sure as I can tell you the sun will rise tomorrow—if you surf the Internet, you will be caught by your wife. If you have an affair, you will be caught by your wife. If you fool around, you will get caught.

This is my one and only piece of advice: get a divorce. Do it now. You *will* be discovered. Better a controlled crash than an out-of-control crash. It will hurt others less if you reveal your sexuality on *your* terms. Yes, it will still hurt. However, to have your friends, family, and co-workers find out by rumor, gossip, or accident that you are gay, or worse yet, by someone finding you in some "compromising situation" at a time and place you can't decide will hurt you and them even more.

That is the worst option of all. It's March of 2003. I'm on standby at Pier 28 along the waterfront in San Francisco. Back in the 1940s, this pier saw sailors heading off for war. Now the pier and the covered warehouse sit virtually empty. The SFPD is using the pier, which is owned by the Port Authority, to stage several platoons of officers for crowd control. At the beginning of this week, the United States invaded Iraq—Gulf War Two. For the last few days, we have been moving around the city and arresting groups of antiwar protestors, both small and large, that are blocking intersections and businesses. The only nice thing about this week so far is that I'm on overtime, and I have gotten to knock a protestor over a newsstand with my riot baton when they swarmed some officers trying to hold onto a prisoner.

At 11:00 a.m., my cell phone rings. Norma is on the phone, but she isn't making much sense at all. What I do know is that she is in the bedroom, and she has fallen. More ominous than that is that she says she can't feel the left side of her face, and her left side is paralyzed. I'm hoping it isn't what I think it is. I'm hoping it's not a stroke. She's only forty-six. I make a call to our local fire department and ask them to get to my home code three and to make forced entry. I'm too far away to be there in time to let the paramedics in, and I don't want to waste time. Doors can be fixed. I tell my captain what is going on, and before I know it, his unmarked city police vehicle pulls up. The captain's aide jumps out and says, "Go." I thank my boss and jump in the car, quickly making progress across the Bay Bridge with my emergency lights on and siren blaring. I arrive at the hospital, still in my riot gear, just as the medics pull into the emergency room entrance. When they open the door of the rig, I am happy to see that Norma is at least smiling.

Oddly enough, during the next thirty minutes, the symptoms went away. Norma's speech and motor function returned. The doctors diagnosed the event as a TIA, which, in layperson's terms, is a stroke caused by a very small clot. In this case, the clot cleared itself, and blood flow returned. It didn't disappear without consequences, however, because after a few weeks, it was clear that Norma's mental function had taken yet another hit. We were now at the point where any conversation was difficult. Norma has no trouble talking. Norma will talk until the cows come home. Her ability to create and communicate thoughts, ideas, and words was wrecked—had been wrecked—since her brain tumor was removed fifteen years before. Now it was even further diminished.

If you ask Norma to read a newspaper article, she can read it. She understands the words. If you ask Norma what the article was about, she can't tell you. Tell her a story, an account of your day, and she listens politely. Unfortunately, she forgets the story immediately. If Norma were a computer, she would be one without any RAM, without the short-term memory we all utilize in the here and now, in the present. It's horribly frustrating for her and for me, and I'm simply not a patient person. I tend to be intellectual. I love arguing politics, current events, and philosophy. Norma, now intellectually functioning at an early grammar school level, was not able to keep up. I was frustrated and short tempered with her, she was mad at me, and both of us were mad at the unfairness of it all. We still loved one another, but the woman I married was gone. I was living with a ghost, a shell, of the lady I married.

It's 9:45 a.m. April 21, 2004. Norma calls me in from the other room. "Peter, we need to talk!" For the millionth time in the last several years, I feel ill. I'm in constant fear of the discovery that my backpacking and skiing buddy is not *just* a backpacking and skiing buddy. I have maintained a long relationship with Mark. I have been seeing him since 1998. When possible, we arranged ski trips or backpacking trips together. We were also having sex. For the last six years, I have been sick with guilt and sick with shame. The constant lying and cheating is taking a terrible toll on me. I know I will be discovered. It is just a matter of time. (The same as you will be discovered.)

The last 999,999 times Norma had exclaimed, "Peter, we need to talk," it was about the bills or the garden or some other mundane thing. Every time I hear the words, "Peter, we need to talk," I'm terrified. But I knew the day was coming. I had dodged bullets over the years. "Peter. Oh boy, we need to talk!" Norma calls again. I walk into the room. Hotmail is open. I had just been in Hotmail writing Mark. I had logged out. I know I did! My letter is open. Norma had hit the "Back" button several times, and each time, the computer said, "This page has expired. Please log back into Hotmail." She hit the "Back" button a few more times and got the same message. "This page is expired. Log back in." She hit the "Back" button over and over. Who would have figured? When she hit the "Back" button one more time, a computer glitch is all it took. There, in my own words, are my "thanks" to my bud for the great time had yesterday … Fill in your own words, readers. It was XXX. There is no way to talk myself out of the letter. I leap across the room and click "Exit." It is too late.

"Peter, what's going on?" The world is a roaring waterfall of noise. I feel as if I have jumped onto an electrified fence. My wife has just found an intimate e-mail from her husband to a man.

"Peter, what's going on?"

"I'm gay," I blurt out, hoping that that one word will explain everything. I had never said that phrase aloud. And then I begin to sob. In self-pity. In loathing. In embarrassment. In shame. In guilt. I had hurt the person who had been promised my love and my companionship until death did us part, in sickness and in health. (It's not epilepsy. You have a brain tumor.) She was now finding out that her life companion in that journey and struggle over the last years was a liar. A betrayer of trust and of love and of goodness.

"This isn't happening! This isn't happening!" is all Norma can scream as I sob in the corner as the noise that sounds like a train crashes through my head. Before that day, I had never uttered those words aloud. "I'm gay."

The next hours were horrid beyond words. They were as black as black could be. If you want me to tell you it went well, I simply can't. It was terrible. I had to tell many people that day what was going on, because I simply couldn't expect Norma not to seek out her family and friends. I had completely shattered her world. I had struck her a terrible blow, one that she had never seen coming. Ultimately, this is a story about coming out in the police department. I can write chapters about the next few days and weeks as I told family and friends the truth. There was simply no way I was going to stay in the closet with family and friends. I didn't have any expectation, nor should I have had any expectations, that Norma was going to keep my secret. Secrets are not things one can expect others to keep, especially when it is the truth. Asking others to hide the truth is to ask others to lie for you. I couldn't do that. I spent the next few days telling my family and friends that I was gay. I had lied. I asked only one thing.

Please don't let this get back to the SFPD. Norma had told me within seconds of finding out the truth that sooner or later I would have to come out at work. I knew that deep in my soul, as well. In that one instant, the thing that I feared most of all, being discovered that I was gay, was neither something that I *could* hide nor something that I *should* hide. I knew that I was going to have to take the medicine. It knew that it was the right thing to do. I would have to come out at work. Right now, I just needed some time before I told work. I asked Norma for the chance to do it on my own terms, when I felt ready. She agreed.

Mark and I had discussed what we would do if we were discovered. Mark has two daughters, at that time eleven and seventeen. If things were complicated for me caring for a wife with a brain injury, things were even more difficult for Mark. Yet both of us knew that this day was coming. We had been close to discovery on several occasions—once when Mark had accidently dialed his cell phone and our conversation was heard by his wife, and once when I dropped a condom wrapper in his "family" boat. Although I had found the condom wrapper before anyone else had, and the conversation Mark's wife had heard was suspicious but not conclusive, we both knew our days in secret were numbered. Both of us had promised if one was discovered that the other would also come out, and we would move in together. In fact, by this time, Mark's wife was well aware that Mark and I were in a sexual relationship. She had simply seen and heard enough, seen how we acted around one another, picked up on enough small clues, that she was convinced what was going on was in fact going on. As a result, she was making Mark's life difficult and nasty. For weeks now, Mark had been telling me, "She knows. She knows." When I called Mark on his cell phone that morning, I wasn't certain he would come out, as well. Mark really had no choice, but in my mind, I still had doubts. Mark told me he was standing in line making a bank deposit when his phone rang. "I'm busted! She knows! She knows!" What Mark remembers more than anything else about that moment is the sound of a train roaring through his head. He then told me what I wanted to hear. He promised that he would stay with me. That Hotmail letter finished a painful period in my life that lasted six years.

I spent the next several weeks explaining to friends and family that I was gay. It was never easy. I broke Norma's heart. I shattered my father-in-law's belief in me. I had to tell my best friend that I was gay. I had to tell my dad. I had to tell a lot of people. Mostly what I was telling them was that I had deceived and lied to them. I was ashamed of myself. To a person, my family and friends were all understanding and supportive. They wanted me to be happy. To a person, they warned me that sooner or later, I would have to be out at work. They didn't see me as being happy if I continued to lie.

Norma and I lived together for several more months, sleeping in separate beds. We tried to ease out of our living situation slowly, but within a few months, Norma told me that it was just too painful for her. I had to move out. Mark and I rented an apartment. Mark became ill when the rental contract was placed in front of him. Whereas I was abandoning an ill wife, Mark was abandoning his two daughters, aged seventeen and eleven. If it was hard for me, it was doubly hard for him.

I came to work one afternoon when an old-timer cop named Frank approached me in the platoon commander's office. It had been two years since my wife Norma found out that I'm gay. I had worked together with Frank back when I was a rookie at Potrero Station. Over the years, I had worked with or supervised Frank, and he is not only a great cop but a great storyteller. When Frank approaches you and exclaims, "Hey, did I tell you the one about ..." you know you are in for an amazing tale and a nice chuckle. You know, at the very least, that you are going to have to suffer having Frank tell you the story at his own pace. Frank's pace is slow. Very, very slow. He draws out every syllable, every nuance, and every detail of a story in living color. He is quite entertaining. The only problem is that he takes forever to tell a story, and if you dare interrupt him, he replies with, "I'm getting to that part." Interrupting Frank only causes him to rewind his story two minutes, serving as a warning to you not to interrupt again. "Hey, Pete, did I tell you what happened to me last night at Whole Foods Bayside?"

"No, Frank, what happened?" I replied, wondering if this story could be kept to less than ten minutes because I really wanted to get my radio car loaded and ready in case the shit started popping.

Red flag! I had been with Mark last night at Whole Foods Groceries, and I was wondering how I could explain buying groceries with another man. "So there I was, in the parking lot, ya know. Just parking my car. Ya know?" Frank says "ya know" a lot, and you have to acknowledge each and every one of them to keep the story moving forward. If you don't acknowledge "ya know," he will sit there and wait. So you have to reply, "Uh-huh," but you have to be careful not to actually interrupt. "Uh-huh, Whole Foods," I replied.

"Parking my car. And I look across the parking lot, ya know?"

"Yuh-huh," I replied, now getting a little concerned.

"And what do I see but these two *fags*, ya know?" Except Frank pronounced "fags" like it had six a's, and it was all in capitals. Frank has a slight East Coast accent, so it came out as "faaaaaggggssss."

"Oh," I mumbled. What could I say? Now loading up my radio car was the furthest thing from my mind. I could feel my pulse race. I felt sick.

Frank said, "So, I see these two *faaagggs*, ya know?"

"Uh-huh."

Franks went on, "And these two *faaagggs* were walking across the parking lot, ya know?"

"Oh?"

"And it was just you and some other guy." Frank left the sentence there. Hanging. "Yup," I replied while trying to keep a poker face because I was at a loss for what Frank thought he saw or did see.

"I thought it was two *faaagggs,* ya know, isn't that funny? It was just you and some other guy. I thought it was two fags." That was the entire story.

It turned out that Frank hadn't "made me." His instinct was telling him something. Frank's instincts, his cop instincts, his male instincts, had "made me." It confirmed what I already knew. Mark and I were putting off a vibe. I knew that this vibe, which might be missed by civilians, was sooner or later going to be noticed when I least expected it by my cop buddies. Most probably I was going to get "outed" by accident when I least expected it, and I would never see the person who "outed" me. Frank had seen us. His instinct nailed us. Frank dropped it. He just thought it was funny, and he had no hidden meaning to the story. I had dodged a bullet.

From that moment on, I knew I was going to have to come out on my own or be found out. I knew sooner or later that the train would come off the tracks. To be honest, at this point, I was getting exhausted. It wasn't fair to my partner Mark, and it was damaging me. I knew I had to find a way to come out at work.

The SFPD is a large agency, and I had been quite active in the department, both as a street sergeant and as a specialist team sergeant. On top of this, I was an FTO sergeant and was constantly seeing new faces come and old faces go. A typical night watch in the SFPD runs between thirty and forty cops, and a station has about 125–150 cops total. There are ten stations and several dozen specialized units and details. Officers are constantly being moved around. Recruits go through three training phases over a sixteen-week period, rotating over the three watches. Once they finish, they transfer out, and they are quickly replaced by a new set of recruits, as many as twelve at a time. As this is happening, officers are both coming off of or entering into their first-year probation, and once again, officers face a mandatory transfer of assignments. You can visit a watch, say a night watch, at the Tenderloin station today, and within three years know virtually no one. There is a tremendous amount of turnover in the place. By the late 1990s and early 2000, I had trained or supervised several hundred cops, and although they all remember their "sarge," this sergeant can't possibly remember all of them. If I saw someone on the street, it was very possible that they remembered me but just as likely that I didn't recognize them. Every walk in the city was like walking through a minefield. It is actually impossible for me to spend time in the city without crossing paths with people I know—or, shall I say, who knows me. Many a chance encounter with an on-duty cop requires a peek at their name tag because I can't possibly put the name to the face. If you worked my station, you might have been an integral part of the watch, maybe even worked a steady sector for a year or so. I may have been on hundreds of calls with you, but five years later, if you catch me cold, it's really hard for me to remember your name. I just work with too many cops that come and go. Mark and I would spend a lot of time in San Francisco, as well as the surrounding communities. It was normal for me, without exaggerating, to run into two or three cops a night who I knew or who knew me. What was worse was that for every cop who saw me walking with my partner, there were two or three who saw me who I didn't realize were around. As a result, I had to be careful of letting my guard down and had to be careful not to show Mark familiarity or intimacy.

I went to see an old friend yesterday. I have known him since I was eighteen. Like many grown people, you tend to watch the years slip by, promising to spend more time visiting friends, but you don't do as well as you'd like. I had been out of the closet, but not out at work, for six months. I called my friend. It had been a few years since we had spoken face to face. It was a Sunday. My friend owns a printing business. We are sitting in his workshop. He is showing me how much the equipment has changed over the years, proudly showing me his business, one that he built from the ground up. The place is empty of people. He is talking about his printing business, but I'm hearing very little of it. I need to say "this thing." I'm terrified of three words. The noise of a train roaring through my head has returned at full volume. It would be close to three years before this noise and buzz of having one's life turned upside down would subside. And right now, I'm all buzz and noise, and I'm really getting myself wound up.

Eventually, I manage to work up the nerve to stop my friend in midsentence. "Can we sit down? I need to tell you something."

"Sure, Pete," he says as he grabs two chairs and places them in the middle of the shop. Minutes go by. I try and try. The tears are running down my face.

"What's wrong, Pete?"

"I'm gay. That's why I left Norma. I'm gay."

Smiling and exhaling all at the same time, my friend replies, "Fuck! Is that all? I thought you were dying of cancer!"

"Huh? Cancer? No! I'm fine!"

"Fuck, I thought you were dying!"

"No," I manage to choke out.

My friend asks, "Are you happy?"

"Yes, I am," I reply.

"Then I'm happy, too."

I learned a valuable lesson. If you drag out the conversation, the drama, and the angst too far, you scare people. You really truly scare people. Since then, I have had similar exchanges with friends, all happy to hear that I'm not dying. When you tell people you are gay, don't beat around the bush. These are the words. You need say nothing more. There is *no* magic pill and no way to say it that doesn't make things worse. It just is. "I'm gay." When you decide to tell someone, say nothing else until you say those two words, lest they think you have cancer.

I had fantasies about ways to come out at work, something dramatic. It is late 2007. Mark and I have not only moved in together, but we have purchased a home. Both of Mark's daughters have been told the truth about the reason for their parents' divorce, and they took it well. Mark and I are out to family and friends, but not at work. Not being out at work has been difficult over the last three years. Mark and I avoid the Castro completely because the beat cops or a passing radio car crew might see me. I'm paranoid, and it is hurting our relationship. We are having Sunday brunch one day at a small table for two on Potrero Hill. I don't know how I was acting, but I know I was relaxed and probably being intimate with Mark in ways couples do when they are at brunch. As I get up at the end of the meal to use the restroom, I see that sitting just to my right are two plainclothes vice cops on their meal break. They have been there the entire time. I know one of the cops really well. I stammer out some lame chitchat with them, all the while trying to guess how far I have burned myself. My heart is pounding, and I feel foolish. Foolish and embarrassed was how I felt the rest of the day. I was embarrassed at myself for playing this charade and waiting to become someone's gossip in a radio car. I was foolish to think that I could do this. I had learned a lesson when Norma found that e-mail to Mark. It's better to have a controlled crash than an out-of-control crash. My crash, my outing of myself, was something I wanted to control.

Eventually, I settled upon a path—a mechanism, if you will—to getting "outed" in the police department. Let's face it, guys—if you are reading this right now, you have already decided to come out at work. It took guts on your part to even read this book. You probably keep this book hidden so no one from work can see it. I know how you feel. Having now decided the deed must be done, how do you do the deed? How do you let the department know that you are gay in a professional manner? How do you come out at work? You start a rumor about yourself. When confronted, admit it. That was my plan. Fuck it. I had decided. As far as the closet goes, I'm out of here.

Gay rumors did start about a sergeant. There is a rumor going around the department. The rumor is that a sergeant got divorced because he is gay and moved in with another guy. The sergeant works at my station. The rumor is true except that the rumor is about another sergeant. He's straight. He did just get divorced, but he is straight. I'm the gay one. The rumor got mixed up. Now I'm really feeling like an asshole. My friend is being tarred with a brush meant for me.

Mike is another sergeant I have known for many years. Mike is a top-notch street sergeant. He is one of the best I have ever worked around. Rumors about Mike's sexuality started about ten years ago. I assumed Mike was gay but in the closet. I had heard folks talking about him. No one ever said anything bad. In fact, it was quite the contrary. It was usually "Mike's a good guy" or "He needs to come out" or "No one cares." I had never heard anything bad said about the possibility of Mike being gay. I did hear some displeasure from cops that he wasn't being honest to them. Cops hate dishonesty. It gets you into jail quicker than just about anything. Lie to a cop and here comes Mr. Handcuffs. The cops who knew Mike didn't care that he was gay, but they did care that he was lying about it. I also heard cops reference other cops who were out, and they spoke highly of many of them. The ones they disliked were the ones who couldn't perform on the streets just the same as they disliked straights that couldn't perform well. Blue is more important than pink. They may not like pink, but first a cop is blue.

I knew that if I was so much as seen with Sgt. Mike that rumors would start about me. Sgt. Mike patrols a neighboring district, and it isn't unusual to cross paths and have a cup of coffee. It is unusual to spend too much time with a cop everyone assumes is gay, and men by their nature apply guilt through association. Just being seen too often with Sgt. Mike was going to start rumors and probably by people who didn't like me. I knew that once I chose my path, I would be committed to coming out. I wanted to keep the "rumor period" about me short. I didn't want to become gossip. I didn't have much of a plan, but I knew Sgt. Mike was someone I could trust, and I also knew that once I started outing myself, I would need to stay the course. I promised myself that I wasn't going to stay in the closet. Besides, I had promised Mark. The hide-and-seek in the city every time we went out was damaging our relationship.

I met Mike for dinner, by itself a bit unusual. Since he seemed to know that something was up, I got right to the point. I knew that I needed to tell him that I was gay first and not expect him to first tell me about his private life. I began by apologizing to him that I didn't want to pry into his personal life but that I thought he was someone I could confide in. I told him that I was gay. I asked him if the rumors about him were true. Without missing a beat, Mike told me that he was gay, but in actuality was only just coming out himself. Prior to that, he had been dating other guys and keeping things separate from work, but he realized that things just weren't working—and like me, he simply had gotten to the "fuck them if they don't like it" stage. He was in the midst of coming out himself. Mike had developed a small circle of friends, gay friends, gay cops, all "out" at work to some degree or another. Mike was about a year ahead of me in coming out at work.

Over the next few months, I met more of Mike's friends, and I got comfortable with being known, at least among a couple of gay cops, as being out. I knew that my risk of discovery was getting higher by the day, but that was my plan. I knew that the more I was seen with these people and the more I talked with their friends and co-workers, the more likely it was that I was going to be discovered. I had intentionally allowed this to happen because it prevented me from turning around to go back in the closet. My secret was potentially becoming an open secret, and there was no way I could stop it even if I wanted to, and I didn't want to. I wanted to get to the point where I had to come out or get "outed" by gossip, something I wanted to avoid at all costs. It was a thin line to walk. Long ago, I had promised myself that if I was confronted at work, I wouldn't lie anymore. If asked by anyone at any time, I was going to tell them that I was gay. I was as ready as I was ever going to be. Over the last few months, I had been seen with Mike too many times. I wanted to come out. I wanted to pull the trigger. I wanted to start a rumor, or rumors, that Sgt. Thoshinsky, Mr. Specialist Sergeant, is gay. There was only one problem. No one was going to ask me. Not in a million years. Call it fear or call it respect; it just wasn't going to happen.

"Hi, everyone! Over here! Merry Christmas!" the queer falsetto voice echoed down the quiet suburban street. It is December 2007, and I have just finished parking my car. My partner Mark is by my side. I'm doing something that just a year ago seemed preposterous. I'm attending a Christmas party with my lover at the home of a host I don't know, with guests that I don't know, but who I understand know people I know, with the specific intent of outing myself by getting a rumor started. "Heterosexual suicide." The plan for this evening had started two months ago when my friend Sgt. Mike was kind enough to invite me to a fellow officer's home for their annual Christmas party. The host, an openly gay police officer in a neighboring jurisdiction, lives with his partner, also a gay police officer. Other than my friend Mike and my partner Mark, I won't know a soul. What's significant is that although I won't know any people at the party, many of the guests attending are friends of people in my agency. I'm well aware of this. I'm aware that if I introduce Mark as "my partner," within days the news will have spread through the SFPD that I'm gay. That was the point of coming here. Now, however, I want to turn and run. I have parked the car, and Mark and I are looking at the address of the home I had written down. The house is totally dark. If there is a party, it isn't tonight.

"Hey! Over here! Merry Christmas!" sings the falsetto male voice again. He—if it *is* a he—is across the street standing in front of a house. I had written the house number down wrong. That must be the place.

This oh-so-gay greeter is giving me doubts about being here. What a fag!    "You still want to do this? I'll support you either way. It's up to you," says Mark.

"No. It's the right thing to do. It's the truth," I replied. My heart was pounding so loudly that I thought I was going to die. I'm thinking to myself, *For Christ's sake, you will run up the stairs to go to a "221" (man with a gun), but you won't go to a Christmas party as an openly gay man? What a pussy! Are you embarrassed to be gay? No, I'm not embarrassed to be gay! Then what? What then? Just start walking. One step at a time. Left. Right. Don't look beyond that. Walk up the sidewalk. Go in the house.* Often the right thing is the hardest to do.

It didn't take long to find the right person to out me, nor did it take long for word to get around. After meeting the hosts of the party and exchanging chitchat, Mark and I moved out to the patio, cocktails in hand. The host made a brief introduction for Mark and me to a nice-looking young lady. As usual, the pleasantries began with, "What do you do?" and "Who do you know?" I introduced the lady to Mark as my partner and gave her a little background on who I knew that might be mutual friends. I had, up until now, never introduced Mark as my partner. I was pretty proud of myself. For five seconds. Beaming and smiling, she replied, "Oh, then you must know Jack Steward? I'm best friends with his wife Anna!" I work with Jack Steward. Not only is he assigned to my station, but he is a member of the specialist team. His wife, Anna, is also an SFPD officer and also a former co-worker. I have been here less than five minutes. I'm now totally and completely out. There is no going back anymore. By talking to this lady, I might have just as well as painted the word "fag" across my forehead and walked into the station. I don't hear another thing the rest of the night. We stayed a while. We left. I didn't feel good, but I didn't feel bad. I had lit the fuse.

I wasn't due back at work for two weeks. I didn't plan it that way; it just so happened that we were spending New Year's at my sister's in Oregon. So really, how much can a girl cop gossip in two weeks? Apparently, quite a bit, because while I was away in Oregon for the Christmas holiday, I was later told that I had stood up at afternoon lineup (roll call) and told everyone that I was gay. My actions apparently pissed off a lot of cops for doing it like that. Officers didn't appreciate me bringing my private life into the workplace. Except that it never happened. I was in Oregon. It is years later, and I still haven't figured out where that "coming out at lineup" story came from. It seems no one wants to hear the truth about how I came out at a Christmas party. They seem to like the idea that I did it at lineup. Oh well.

January 6, 2008. I spent the last two weeks on vacation. I haven't been at work since the Christmas party. At our station, the sergeants arrive one hour before the patrolmen, giving the sergeants an opportunity to get briefed by the previous supervisors and generally get up to speed on what events are occurring in the district. I have been in the platoon commander's office less than one minute. 3:01 p.m. Jason, a fantastic sergeant, a friend, and a wonderful guy, suddenly walked past the open door of the platoon commander's office and glanced in. There is a long-established Irish Catholic hierarchy in the department. The command staff of my station is strongly rooted in that culture. Virtually all of the lieutenants and sergeants are Irish Catholic, and although I don't care much about their religion, the sergeants and lieutenants I work with are fantastic cops and people whose friendship and respect I'm hoping to keep. Jason, in my mind, is an important element in that group. He is someone who I hope will treat me the same as he always has and who will be supportive of me, gay or straight. The time has come to find out if that is going to happen.

Jason is peeking around the doorjamb and looking directly at me. Something is up.

"Dude, we need to talk!" says Jason. Jason is all smiles, but he obviously wants to talk about something significant. I want to be done with this already. I desperately want someone to finally ask me! We walk down the hall and pause in a private area of the station. "So," says Jason, getting right to it. "There's this rumor going around. I'm going to tell you that I don't care either way. This makes no difference to me, but I think you should know. There are some people talking smack about you here, saying you are gay. I don't care if you are gay, but I do care that guys are talking smack about you, and I'm going to kick their ass."

"It's true," I reply.

"Well, they are really talking shit. I don't like it. I'll smack 'em," is Jason's reply. He's still not catching on. It's out of left field for him.

"It's true. I'm gay."

"You're gay?" he asks me again.

"Yup." There is a pause. Then in typical Sgt. Jason style, he beams a big smile, parks a big ugly wad of tobacco chew in his gums, and asks, "Are you happy? Because if you are happy, goddamn it, then I'm happy. So, are you happy?"

I tell him that I am. Then he offers to kick the shit out of anyone who talks smack about me.

Somehow I made it through the swing watch lineup, feeling as if everyone now knew that I was a fag and was staring at me. As soon as I could, I loaded up my radio car and hit the streets. I made it a few blocks and pulled over. I have never shed a tear on duty. Off duty, I cry pretty easily, I guess. With a good sad movie or a good sad book, the waterworks turn on. I had never, ever shed a tear while in uniform. I did now. It was finally over. Nothing else happened that day. Within a few minutes, I went back to work, forgetting all together about the issue that had plagued me since puberty. Over the next few days, only one other person broached the subject of my sexuality. A member of the specialist team pulled me aside to let me know that some asshole was spreading rumors that I was gay but that I could count on him to put an end to it. He promised to "kill that rumor."

"Please, don't," I said. "It's true." I had to tell him three more times. When it finally sunk in, he made another offer. He wouldn't let my secret get around. He would punch anyone who said it. I made him promise not to. I wanted him to tell whoever he wanted to. I wanted him to tell everyone he could that I was gay. I didn't care anymore. I was done.

The next few weeks at work were very strange. It was strange because *nothing* happened. Strange because I made the mistake of assuming that *everyone* had heard the news. They hadn't, my importance to the police department being not nearly as significant as my ego thought it was. Believing that the rumor mill had done its work already several times, and thinking that I owed some friends an explanation, I brought up the subject myself.

More often than not, I started off the conversation with something like "I guess you heard rumors about me." Surprisingly, the answer to the question many times was "no." Many times I was left standing there awkwardly and forcing myself to say something like "Well, there's a rumor going around that I'm gay. It's not a rumor. It's true." Each and every time, I got one of two answers. Usually, it was "Really? Oh," The other answer, if the person had heard the news, was, "Makes no difference to me."

I learned a few things over the next few weeks. It turned out that several officers I knew were gay, including a veteran motorcycle sergeant. In addition, other cops were frequenting gay bars and being seen by other gay officers, but no one cared. The dread I felt about being seen with Mark in the Castro, for instance, wasn't necessary. Gay cops, having suffered "the life" themselves, were simply too respectful of one another to tell anyone. The exposure to ridicule and rumors that seemed so scary to me and kept me awake all night was all in my head. The only person in the San Francisco Police Department who had a problem with me being gay was me. The only person who was ashamed of being gay was me. It was all for nothing. It has been a little over two years since I came out at work. The fallout has been nil, virtually nonexistent. As I proceeded further into my career and took on more responsibilities, I convinced myself and I firmly believed that if I came out of the closet, my accomplishments would be tarnished, that I would be revealed as a "faker." As irrational as it sounds, I had wrapped up my sexuality with every single thing that I did. I believed that my manhood, my courage, and most importantly, my ability to lead would be suddenly called into question if it was discovered that I was gay. I was wrong. It was all in my head. People are so busy leading their own lives that your sexuality will fall from their radar almost right away. We are all adults here, and to gossip about a guy being gay is viewed upon with distain if carried too far. All straight men naturally shy away from talking about "gay" too much, knowing that too much talk will have others wondering why the speaker is so interested.

In an odd turn of events, the strength of the EEO laws are such that discussing the personal lives of co-workers has become almost taboo. The sexual harassment and discrimination laws make it difficult for friends in the workplace, even well-meaning friends, to openly question your sexual orientation. Let's face it, though. If your work persona and reputation are beyond reproach, no one will have the guts to ask you. Why would they? If you are so established, so deep into being the cop that you are, no one is going to say a word. To your face. You can't control what others say behind your back. The best you can hope for is that what they say is the truth.

Each reader of this story knows how much exposure they have had of being discovered. If you are married, then most probably your activities have made you venture out of the home to see guys. You have even more exposure if you are single, because people are already wondering why you aren't dating anymore. You think you are being seen by co-workers, or will be seen, or will never be seen, but what difference does that make? You firmly believe that you are on the verge of discovery by now. That might be true; that might not be true. What is true is that you are reading this book. You are reading this story. Right now.

What is true is that you can take one of two paths at this stage in your life. You can remain in the closet and risk discovery and ridicule— ridicule you will never hear but can only imagine. Your paranoia will grow. You will be unhappy. Some of you are considering suicide. More than a few. Pussy. There, I said it. Man up.

My wife Norma and I moved into separate homes in 2004, me with Mark and Norma in her own place. In a silver lining in an otherwise dismal surgical outcome, Norma discovered that she had an untouched artistic side of her brain, the right side, which functions quite well. Norma's surgery had been to the left side of her head, the intellectual portion of the brain. Emotion and art reside together in the right side of your head. Art and emotion are an expression of one another, deeply intertwined. When Norma is in an emotional discussion, for instance, one with a lot of anger, she speaks perfectly. The real discovery was her talented print making, utilizing traditional etched plates, paper, and press. Her work has won awards, including a recent first-place award in Solano County. She hasn't gotten over the pain and anger of my betrayal of her trust. She remains terribly hurt, but she is a tough lady, and she deals with life as it comes. Her art provides an outlet for her, a place to go where one doesn't need words to speak eloquently. In the meantime, I do my best to be there for her. I know that isn't enough, but it's the best I can do.

I get the "handshake" a lot. It goes like this. I'll be walking to the radio car in the station parking lot or down the halls in the Hall of Justice. An officer who I haven't seen in a long period will come over and say hi and shake my hand. Not unusual. I have provided the reader *italics* to provide you a translation of "the handshake." It goes like this:

Greeter: "Hey, Pete, how ya doing?" The greeter extends a hand. *(Hey. I haven't seen Pete since I heard he's gay. I wonder how he is doing).*

Me: "Good. Real good." Or "Fine, considering how fucked up this day has been." You get the picture. I'm shaking hands and going through social pleasantries when it naturally comes time to, well, stop shaking hands. It's time to let go.

Greeter: "You doing okay?" *(Are you getting harassed by cops since you came out?)*

Me: "Sure, great. How have you been?" Shake-shake, clasp hand for emphasis.

Greeter: "Good. Good. So, everything's okay, then? They treating you good here at Southern?" *(Man, that's got to be tough being a gay cop and all).* Shake-shake. (Uh, I need my hand back.)

Greeter: "So everything's okay? Well, good, I'm happy to hear that." *(I'm surprised, actually; these cops can be dicks sometimes.)*

Me: "Thanks. I appreciate that." Tug. Shake.

Greeter: "Well, I'm happy to hear you're getting along." *(I'm happy no one is giving you a hard time. It makes no difference to me that you are gay).* Release me!

Some of these "handshake interactions" have been quite lengthy. They never fail to make me smile. It shows that friends care. To those who have done this long handshake thing, I say, "Thank you! To have people continue to stop and shake your hand like they did when you were straight, whether or not the message you are sending is real or just in my own head, means more than you can imagine."

My road has had some bumps since I came out. Some people, and it's an extremely small number, ignore me. They do what they need to do when we are on an assignment, but otherwise these people avoid me. If I'm directing officers to do something, or if they are backing me up, they always perform their duties. In June of 2009, I walked in uniform representing the SFPD in the San Francisco Gay Pride Parade, and I'll do it again next week. I walked down Market Street with my partner Mark through all my police haunts. The Southern, the Central, the

Northern, the Mission, and Tenderloin police districts. I don't walk for myself. I walk for the cop in the closet. I walk for you.

Enough about me; let's talk about you. You didn't accidentally purchase this book. The mere fact that you are reading this leads me to but one conclusion. You want to come out of the closet. You are seeking a path. First off, if you are embarrassed to be gay, get over it. You have nothing to be embarrassed about. If you can't stop feeling embarrassed, coming out will be that much harder. I hate to sound like a sound byte, but you need to stand tall. I'm not saying become some flag-waving activist, but you should be at the point where you are ready to look *anyone* square in the eye and say, "I'm gay."

By now, you have either come close to being discovered or think you have been close to being discovered several times. The anxiety and worry is the same whether that is true or not. The odds are that your wife suspects. We won't dive into all the psychological trauma and unhappiness you are suffering; that's a whole other topic deserving of someone more qualified than I.

If you are married, you must get a divorce. The reasons you use, the excuse you give your wife or husband, is not nearly as important as the fact that the marriage must end. You are gay.

That isn't going away. It is not a phase. You are gay. It's time to get a divorce. From then, the speed at which you go from divorce to "out" in the workplace is up to you. I think you should first take a little time in coming out to family and friends, but again, that's a topic for a whole other book.

After you come out, never again deny that you are gay. I want you to imagine how much courage it takes for someone to ask *you* if you are gay. That is not a question a friend or colleague asks lightly, especially if you are an "alpha male" well into an "alpha male" career. In this modern day workplace of EEO and sexual harassment laws, I think it is harder to come out, and although the protection of these laws far outweighs the undesired consequence, it is just about impossible to discuss issues of sexuality in the workplace. Even if it isn't a violation of law or policy, it's "sex." People are not comfortable talking about sex. Besides, sex really doesn't belong in the workplace. Of course, sex is in the workplace.

Men wrap themselves in masculinity and equate that to their sexuality and thus into the job—most especially in policing.

You being gay or straight didn't make you into the cop or man you are. It is simply not true. What is true is that your deeds—the deeds you have accomplished and the deeds you will accomplish—are what make you a good cop. The past cannot be taken away from you, and those deeds cannot be undone. You are not trying to change your past. You are trying to change your future. Are people going to laugh and chuckle behind your back? Maybe. Probably. Get over it. I hear cops talk about gay cops that are in the closet. I have heard it for years. Locker room and radio car blabber. They all say, "I just wish he would come out. Nobody cares (or everyone knows)." Implied in those statements, and many times spoken aloud, is how cops hate being lied to and deceived by fellow officers. We are lied to so often that we begin to believe that everyone lies all the time, if for nothing better than to make themselves look more heroic or, in many cases, innocent. Victims embellish and suspects deny. As a result of being constantly lied to by the public, cops really hate it when they are deceived by other men in blue.

If someone asks you if you are gay, recognize it as what it is—an olive branch. If you are an established officer with a good reputation, very little should change for you at work. My method for coming out on the job was to "force my own hand" by putting the truth out in the form of gossip so it would then come back to me as a rumor. I had decided months before that I would admit my sexuality at the very first opportunity.

If you have openly gay officers in your agency, maybe this is the time for you to be seen with them. Not only will you have someone for support, but it begins the process in a small but critical way. For me, having coffee alone with Sgt. Mike was the ignition source to coming out at work. Just simply being seen with him was sure to start rumors, or at the very least I thought it would start rumors. This "being gay thing" is mostly all in *your* head. My belief that I was being seen and talked about may have been paranoia, but it did push me along to do what I knew needed to be done. I firmly refused to take one single step backward. In the end, it's something you alone must do. Only you can say the words "I'm gay" aloud.

I was fortunate in that I stumbled upon a bold manner to out myself—by me being invited along with my partner to a Christmas party hosted by another bunch of cops not in the SFPD. If it had been a party attended solely or wholly by members of my agency rather than by a group of people on the fringes of my work relationships, I don't think I would have done it. At some point, you will feel safe and secure enough to tell another straight officer the truth. Ultimately, unless you get discovered by fate, there is no other way to reveal that you are gay. No podium or soapbox exists in our society within the workplace that affords a forum for such discussions. Tell a co-worker. Tell someone you know will support you that you are gay. There is no way around that. One day, you will be able to say, "I don't want it being a secret anymore."

A few months ago, I was hauling my gear through the station. Assault carbine, gear bag, baton, tag book. I trundled out the back door and loaded up the black-and-white. After setting up and logging into the computer, I reviewed the pending calls for service and the status of the sector cars on the computer terminal. I saw that there was nothing pressing. I had some paperwork to do, so after cracking the windows to keep the radio car from overheating in the sun, I went back inside. Young cops, as a rule, do not speak to me except as part of their duties. This is especially true of probationary officers. I'm a very senior sergeant. People say I look mean. Whatever. I sometimes don't appear approachable. Young officers are always shy around me.

There is a probationary officer waiting at the door in the hallway. I don't know his name. He isn't on my shift, and we don't overlap on our hours. As I get closer, it is clear that he needs to speak to me. I know it isn't about approving booking charges, because he checked off shift fifteen minutes before. So I know what is coming.

"Sgt. Thoshinsky, do you have a minute? I want to ask you something." He is nervous and obviously trying to keep his nerve. He blurts it out. "How do you keep your personal life and work life separate? You seem so good at it. How do you keep them apart?"

"Keep them separate? You mean being gay and work?" I reply.

"Uh-huh," is his reply, and he seems to calm down a little since I have said the word "gay" for him.

"I don't. I don't keep them apart. They have absolutely nothing to do with one another. I don't try; it just is. There is nothing to keep apart."

We talk. He is gay and in fact was open about it at his previous job. When he joined the department, he went back into the closet. He felt that it would be impossible to be successful at establishing a reputation if he was known to be gay. The fact that I had an intact reputation led him to believe that he could do the same. I told to him, and I will you now, this truth: a cop is known by his deeds, not by who he sleeps with. Ultimately, the deeds you do and the tasks you perform—your performance on the job—are the only things that counts.

Blue before pink.

# RICHARD J. SWALLOW

Since I am not ghostwriting, you all know my name. So with that said, I would like to fill you in on that before I go into my story.

I am a twin. No, my twin is not gay since I am always getting asked that. When we were born, my parents did not know they were having twins. It was supposed to be just one. To their surprise, they got two of us. We were premature like most twins. The doctor told them that they did not think we were going to make it, so if they had names picked out, it would be best to name us. They had a name picked out for just one—Brian Richard. Since my twin was born first, he got the name Brian. So any cop can figure out that I got the shaft and got Richard. I do joke about my name and sometimes tell my friends, "Just think of it this way—if I ever wanted to do porn, I would not have to change my name."

Growing up, I lived in a small town in the region. For those who are not from Indiana, the region is its own world. Gary, Indiana, was my neighbor, as well as Chicago. Later in life, I would start my police career in my hometown as a reserve officer and later as a part-time officer.

As a kid, I always knew that I wanted to be a cop. I remember riding around on my *CHiPs* motorcycle. I remember making handcuffs out of my construction set. I knew what I wanted to do for a living at an early age.

It was not 'til my freshman year in high school that I realized that I was gay. I did not know what to do. I went to a Catholic high school. So right there, I knew it would not be okay. Our sex education class consisted of a priest saying, "A penis does not fall from the sky and land in a vagina." So, I did not have anyone to talk to. I did not know anyone who was gay, let alone a gay cop. So I made a decision right then in there; I would play it straight.

I graduated high school and went to college. You guessed it. I still played it straight in college. Once I graduated college, I knew it was going to be tough getting on a department. I had already heard that it was who you know regardless of whether you are the best candidate. Within three months of being out of college, I got hired on part time as a juvenile detention officer with a local county and later went full time with them. Right after that, I got hired on with my hometown police department as a reserve officer.

My dream was starting to come true. After being on as a reserve for not that long, I remember getting pulled into the chief's office. I was nervous as can be because I did not know what was going on. He asked if I was interested in becoming a paid officer. I said yes. So everything was starting to fall in place. The only problem I had at this department was the fact that I still looked like I was in high school. On several occasions, dispatch received calls asking if they knew that a kid had stolen one of their police cars.

At no time was I ever questioned about my sexual orientation. Shortly after that, I got on my current department, the Indiana State Excise Police. For those of you that do not know Indiana, we have four state police agencies—the state troopers that are in charge of the highways and firearms, the conservation officers that are in charge of wildlife and water, the gaming officers that are in charge of casinos and illegal gambling outside of bars, and finally, my department, the Indiana State Excise Police, which is in charge of alcohol and tobacco.

My department mostly deals with bars, restaurants, liquor stores, underage drinking parties, juveniles purchasing tobacco, drugs, public nudity, and so on. Because of the types of investigations that we do, we typically do not wear uniforms, and we drive unmarked cars.

My first day of recruit school was interesting. I did not know what to expect. One of the first questions I was asked was, "What were your parents thinking when they named you?" Through our recruit school, the seven of us were pretty close. One of the guys in my recruit school was also going to my same district. I thought we were friends, but later I would find out otherwise.

Once I got off of FTO, I reported to my district. Unlike the other officer that was going to my district, I was trained outside of the district I would be working in. My FTO and his ex-wife, who is also on the department, would later become two of my closest friends and still are.

When I reported to my district, I was in for a different world. I was restricted in what I could do. I was no longer able to be proactive. I was told, "If you do not have a complaint on a place, you should not be there." Not too long after that, I was dealing with a bar owner. We had raided his bar. Needless to say, we arrested his underage daughter, who was in his bar and had been drinking, and numerous other minors. That did not sit well with him. I explained to him that once I was done doing what I was doing, I would speak with him. Needless to say, he interrupted me continuously. It was not until he was walking away that he called me a "fucking faggot." I brushed it off. But he continued to say it. Finally, I'd had enough. No officer there stepped in to correct the behavior. I was not out yet. But up until now, I had never allowed *any* officer I worked with to be degraded. All of the officers present allowed it to happen. I was not going to let it. I walked outside where the bar owner was. I asked if he had a problem with me or any officer there. He responded, "No." Once I heard that, I walked away.

That night, I think I came out without meaning to because of my actions. Not too long after that, I was called down to headquarters, which was about a two-and-a-half-hour drive to Indianapolis, because of my dealings with the bar owner. I was told that I would be attending "Tactful Communications when Dealing with Difficult People." My immediate thought was, *Are you serious? You are sending me to anger management because a bar owner called me a "fucking faggot"?* When a bar owner in the past called an officer a nigger or a bitch, it was not tolerated. That bar owner was made to write an apology to the officer. But I did not get any of that. I took it and walked out the door.

I feared being the only cop at the class. I was not! There was another cop there, plus a wife of a cop. I explained why I was there, but I left off the "faggot" part. I had their support. It was nice. When I completed my class, I started to notice that things had changed. I went down to another district to assist with a big detail. The car I was in was tagged with a rainbow sticker. I brushed it off and wanted to say, *Are you serious? I do not even like the rainbow.* Upon getting back from that detail, I now noticed that I was working alone when scheduled with other officers. I would call the other officers that I was scheduled to work with, but they would either say they had nothing to do, which was not true, or they would not answer their phones. I would find out later from another gay cop who they did not know was gay that they told him they refused to work with me because I was a faggot. Mind you, at this point, no one had asked me if I was gay or not, nor did I say that I was gay.

I brought it up to my district commander that they refused to work with me. I was told by him that he would address it. To this day, I do not know if it was addressed or not. About a week went by, and nothing had changed, so I brought it up to my district commander again. This time, the response was different. I was told that one officer was leaving the department and that I should try to wait it out. Once the officer left, I was pretty much on my own. The other officer refused to work with me.

Summer came that year, and it was my birthday. My sister-in-law asked me what I wanted to do. I said, "Let's go to the gay bar in town." That night changed my life. Part of me did not want to hide who I was anymore. Mind you, I had not come out to anyone. I told her that we were going there to have fun. The other bars in my district knew who I was and did not care for an excise officer coming in to drink off duty.

I met a cop there that night. He knew who I was, but I did not remember him. One of my friends came up to me and said, "There is a cop here. He knows what department you are on. He asked if you were gay, and I said no, but he still wants to talk to you." I asked her what department he was on. She told me. So, I went up to him and talked to him. I pretended like I remembered him. I told him that I thought I had recognized him and said what department he was on. It was the night that I decided I had put my career first for too long. I was going to live my life and not let the job rule me. We were talking and dancing, and then he asked me if I was gay. I said, "Yes, but no one knows." We both smiled at each other and kept talking and dancing.

Later that night, I walked my sister-in-law out to her car because she was ready to leave, but I was not ready to leave. For the first time in a long time, I felt free and alive. When we got to her car, she brought my choice of bar up. I told her something to the effect that I was having fun and gave her a look. She smiled, and I smiled back. That was all that was said that night about it.

After that, I went back and continued to go back. I was living my life for the first time. I was nervous about who was going to find out and how they would react. So I figured it was time to start coming out to people.

One night, I called an officer that I used to work with at my first department. We were best friends now and shared everything with each other even though we had gone to different departments. She asked if everything was okay. I said I was not sure but I needed to talk to her. She was out at a bar and knew I needed to talk. She got to my house so quickly that I was not prepared on how I was going to tell her. I took her outside on my deck and told her I had been lying to her. She asked me what about. I told her that I was afraid what I was about to tell her would ruin our friendship. She promised me that whatever I said would not. I told her that I was gay. She gave me a big hug. Once she let go, she made it a point to let me know that she loved me and nothing would change our friendship. After she said that, she said something to the effect that she wanted to know what she needed to do as my "fag hag." She asked if my family knew, and I told her that I wanted to wait until I met someone before I told them. Shortly after that, I did meet someone.

It was time to tell my family and close friends. But some of them beat me to the punch. I was confronted with it. I felt betrayed a bit. This is something that I wanted to tell them. I wanted to be the one that said, "I am gay," not "I heard a rumor. Is it true?" When it came time to tell my mom and dad, I was scared shitless. I had always been close with them and was so afraid. I did not want to lose that. When I told them that I was gay, they said they loved me and have always wanted me to be happy.

After that, my mom brought up my job. She said that she was afraid for me. She had heard stories about gay cops not having backup when they needed it. I assured her that who I told at work was my decision. I was not going to come jumping out at work with a rainbow flag saying that I was gay. I reassured her that I would be okay at work even though I had known already that it was not okay at work. My life went on, and I continued working alone most of the time. I missed being active.

A year or so went by 'til I got my chance to be active again. We had a class of about thirty officers that we hired. We needed FTOs. I saw this as my chance to be active again and train the new officers to be proactive. I put in to be an FTO and got it. While I was at FTO school, we had a scenario to complete. It involved a gay person and as well as straight people. During the training, a comment was made which, in a nutshell, was "Why would we pick a gay person? They cannot do anything for us." Also during the FTO school, it was made known to me that the officer I was supposed to room with at the academy during the school was beyond happy that I had gotten a hotel room. He made it clear that he did not want to room with me because I was gay.

FTO school was complete, and now I just had to wait for new officers to graduate. While waiting for that to happen, something major happened involving another officer and myself. One night, an officer from another district—he knew I was gay—and I had to go in undercover to a bar. Needless to say, the shit hit the fan that night. We were working a multiagency detail that night. We requested immediate assistance due to us being in trouble and not having any duty gear on us. We needed immediate backup. Upon requesting it, we were told no by my new district commander. Once all the agencies had arrived at our location, the officer and I had one suspect in custody thanks to an off-duty reserve officer I knew who had helped us. Two other people had fled in a car, and another had fled on foot. The one in custody had blood all over him, as did I. The district commander, upon getting out of the vehicle, was not concerned about our well-being or that of the prisoner. We were told to take the prisoner to the van and get inside and help.

Later that night, I found out that our request for help was never communicated to any other agency involved. I was told by officers that if they had known, they would have responded appropriately.

To this day, I truly do not know why she did not communicate that officers were in need of emergency assistance. Would it have been different if I were not involved? I hope my being gay was not the issue. I would never want another officer that worked with me to be denied assistance or backup because they were working with me. After that, we got a new district commander.

I was not sure how much he knew about me, but if it had not trickled down to him that I was gay, it would.

One night, the guy I was with for almost three years and I had gone out. To this day, I am not sure what triggered the events of that night, because prior to coming home, we had an awesome night out with friends. We had come home and were both hungry. I started cooking something I wanted to eat. He was not happy about it. I finished cooking what I wanted. I went into the bedroom and was going to eat it. He came into the room, ripped the plate out of my hands, and threw it into the wall. I pushed him out of the bedroom because I knew that what was coming was bad, and I locked the door. Needless to say, he broke the door down. By the end of the whole ordeal, I had had a butcher's knife pressed against my throat and was told he was going to kill me as well as having my head put through two doors.

Needless to say, the local police department showed up. I made the phone call to my district commander saying that I needed to talk so I could let him know what happened. When he returned my call, I did not know what to expect. I was afraid and ashamed. I got a return call. When I explained what had happened, I was asked if I was okay and if I needed anything. When I said I needed a few days off to take care of things, I was told to take as much time off as I needed. Before ending our conversation, he reminded me that I could call him at anytime if I needed to talk or needed anything.

Later, I found out that one of the officers that responded that night was not initially okay with gay people. He had told officers that night that he wanted to take me to jail. When asked by the other officers what he would take me to jail for, he told them battery. The other officers stood up for me. They had to make him realize that I was the victim.

To this day, I do not know what I would have done if my duty weapons were not locked my police car. I know that night I did look to my nightstand, which is where I normally kept one of my duty weapons, but once I looked over there, I realized it that was locked up in my squad.

After that night, I was worried about how things would be when I went back to work. Nothing had changed. I was talked about on a regular basis. The comments made by other officers and supervisors throughout the state about gay people were made known to me.

One day, I was called into the superintendent's office about some stuff that had gone on. When I walked into his office, the staff attorney was there. I thought, *Oh, shit, this is not good.* During that meeting, I said everything that had been done to me. Everything I had heard regarding gay people being said by officers and supervisors on this agency was aired out. His first response was, "This is the first time you have told me you were gay."

I wanted to respond, "You know I am; you did not tell me you are African American, but I still know." When he referred to my being gay as a sexual preference and a choice, I almost snapped back, "This is not a preference or a choice. I did not choose to be gay. I would not wish what I had gone through on anyone. Pepsi over Coke is a choice and a preference." Overall, the conversation went extremely well.

Once the conversation was over, he had me go to the Office of Professional Standards to make a complaint. I made the complaint and then left. A couple of days later, I sent the Office of Professional Standards an e-mail with some ideas I had to help stop the homophobia that seemed to be plaguing our department. I suggested diversity training as well as using the Indianapolis Gay Pride Event to promote the department and use it as a recruiting opportunity. The response I got back was that they were already looking into it. I was excited about it. It came time for our state-wide training and banquet like every year. Cultural diversity was not one of the topics, but it later would be.

The first night there set the tone for me for the entire weekend. I was outside with my former FTO's ex-wife. We all were talking when I heard an officer say "Faggotty." I turned to look and to see who said it. When I turned to see who said it, the officer made sure to look me in the eyes, smirk at me, and he said it again. The officer who said it was standing with my former district commander that refused me and the other officer emergency assistance and the other officer who refused to work with me. At this time, I told my FTO's ex-wife that I was going to go back to her room to get something. She knew something was up and came with me. When I told her what had just happened, she was floored. Needless to say, we went back downstairs. I looked at the officer directly in the eyes and asked my FTO's ex-wife if she was having a good time. She said yes. When I asked, "Are you sure you are not having a *fag-tastic* time?" She responded with, "I am having a *gay ole* time." The look on the officer's face was priceless.

The night went on, and I did tell my district commander, who was now my former FTO, what had happened. We talked about it for awhile. When we went to come back in, that same officer was still outside. I found out the next day that while we walked by him, he made a comment that my district commander and I must have been having a sexual relationship.

Training the next day was interesting. Part of it dealt with background investigations. At one point, the instructor, who worked for the federal government, made a comment that there was nothing wrong with hiring a gay person, but if they do not disclose it during the background investigation and you find out, you should not hire them. Needless to say, once I was able to leave, I left.

About a month later, we were mandated to do cultural diversity training. A lot of people were not happy with it. The Indianapolis Gay Pride event was coming up, and I had not heard anything as far as our department participating. I mentioned this to my district commander, and he made a phone call. During the phone call, he was told it that would have to go through the public information officer. So, I forwarded all of the contact information I had on it.

That night, I decided to check my work e-mail before I headed to Chicago to see my boyfriend. The public information officer sent me an e-mail asking why we should participate in the event since the higher-ups wanted justification for it. I typed out, "Can they give me one good reason we should not?" But I deleted that and gave them several reasons—to promote our department, to promote diversity, to promote education when it comes to alcohol and tobacco, and for recruitment possibilities. I also pointed out that we did these types of programs at the state fair, black expo, colleges, local fairs, other minority events, and so on. This should be no different. Finally, I put my little say it in and ended it with the thought that maybe it would force the homophobic officers and supervisors on this agency to realize that it is not going to be tolerated. I had made a complaint about this almost three months ago, and things had not changed. I had an officer look me in the face at our state-wide meeting and say "Faggotty" twice. I went on with a little more.

Instead of getting an e-mail back from the public information officer, I got an e-mail back from the superintendent. The e-mail said that we would not be able to participate at this time. It also asked me to name the officers involved at the state-wide meeting. I emailed him back the names and made it known that my district commander was made aware, and he had also made the Office of Professional Standards aware that night.

Almost a week later, I got a phone call from my roommate letting me know that my work phone had been going off like crazy. I was in Chicago visiting my boyfriend, so I called it and checked my voicemail. The voicemail was from the Office of Professional Standards on behalf of the superintendent asking me to call back as soon as I got the message. I called the Office of Professional Standards and was asked if I would like to come to headquarters and work.

I am now based out of headquarters, and I am happy. Everyone there knows that I am gay and has no issue with that. I have the support I longed for finally after seven years with this agency. Previous stories I have read show that departments can be accepting and open to gay officers as well as gay people. My agency still has its struggles to this day with it and always will. I am not the only gay person on my department anymore. They, too, have faced the struggles that I did earlier on, but not to the extreme that I did.

The only advice I can give to any officer coming out is to do it on your own terms and no one else's. The road you face when you do decide to come out can be a bumpy one. Just remember that you are not alone. There are more of us out there than you think.

# THOMAS BELL

The words "faith" and "hope" mean a lot of different things to different people. To some, they encompass their deepest feelings for those they love—their families, their friends, their communities, or their God. To others, they mean the ability to persevere through unimaginable tragedy in their lives. For me, they are not nouns as much as they are verbs; they are actions that guide my philosophy in life and give me a perspective into my world.

My upbringing certainly guided me to develop this life philosophy. I was raised in the conservative state of Oklahoma and have lived most of my life here. My childhood was not unique from others of my generation in that I had a loving family who faced the reality of divorce, had to make tough decisions to financially survive on more than one occasion, and who moved around from time to time. Although my mother left when I was six, and I have since gone through several stepmothers and stepfathers, I always had a regular core family consisting of my brother, sister, father, and grandmother to guide me through my formative years.

My family was conservative, and I was brought up in the church.

This led me to an understanding of right and wrong, and it was at this early age that I learned that there were some rules to follow in life. I took this logic to heart, and when I started school, I was always known as the "teacher's pet," not so much because I was a kiss-up, but rather because I rarely broke the rules. To me, it always seemed better to do what I was supposed to do because there was a moral imperative to do so. I had faith that if the rules were followed and if I did the right thing, then I could be anything I wanted to be. My father introduced me to a deep understanding of morality at this age when he told me, "Son, right and wrong are simple. Think of it this way: your right to swing your fist stops just short of my face." To me, the yin and yang of liberty versus constraint were so easily realized in this lesson.

As I approached my teenage years, I began to notice that I was somehow different from my friends. I was always amused at this incredible obsession that my buddies seemed to have with the girls around us, and while I had a steady girlfriend, I saw her as much more of a friend than anything else. I hadn't fully realized my attraction to the same sex by that time, and that was due in part to my religious feelings. I had heard teachings in the church about homosexuality, but I attributed my inclinations to confusion, and I assumed that I was just going through a phase.

By the time I entered high school, I began to realize that my feelings toward other guys were becoming stronger. It was about that time that I started to pray that God would keep me from what I considered to be a moral sin. I had faith that my feelings would pass, and I would move on to live a "normal" life. But, in spite of this internal struggle that was brewing inside of me, I managed to enjoy a very happy and healthy life in school, participating in various activities and making wonderful friends that I have to this day. I was able to do this because I never lost sight of my belief that with a little faith and hope in myself and others, everything would come out just fine for me.

I graduated high school and immediately started classes at a state university. It was in college that I was first exposed to a more positive attitude about homosexuality, and I was quite amazed at those around me who were out of the closet and also at the professors who spoke of it as a nonissue. Although I superficially professed to be opposed to homosexuality, I felt much deeper that "those" people were being unfairly characterized as lost and confused. I did meet some out gay people around this time, and I made it a point to not be "preachy" with them. I knew that although I was taught what they were doing was wrong, their fist was not really hitting me in the face. That was probably a good approach for me because it would not be long before I would be in their shoes.

Around my third year of college, I began to slip into a depression. My feelings and attractions toward other guys became overwhelming, and no mater how much I prayed or wanted them to go away, they only became stronger. I had secret crushes every now and then that I wrote off as just deep friendships, and although I began to realize that I was gay, I still thought that it was something that I could control or erase. As my depression deepened, I reached a crossroads; I came to feel that my attractions were out of my control, and if I continued to fight them, I could literally go insane. I started to struggle with insomnia, and my grades began to suffer. My friends and roommates began to notice changes in my behavior, and they grew concerned.

It was around this time that I went for a long walk one night. It was summer, and I remember how warm the air was on campus. A lot of tears began to flow, and I finally got it: I was who I was. My struggle to be something that I wasn't had robbed me of my hope and faith that I had leaned on through my life. It was during that walk that I made a decision to return to myself. I was listening to a song on the radio at the time, and I heard the words "Learn to love yourself … it's a great, great feeling." I realized that I had lost that part of me that was wide eyed and amazed at how wonderful life could be. I realized that while I was already a really good person, what I truly needed was to find my own skin and be comfortable in it. By the end of the walk, I had decided to accept the fact that I was gay. My internal sense of right and wrong had led me to understand that I could never be true to anyone in my life if I couldn't be true to myself first. I knew that I had been deceptive with my feelings about myself and others, and it was time for that to stop. I knew that it was going to be a rough road ahead, but along with my rediscovered faith, my hope in life would begin to return, as well.

After making the decision to start my own coming-out process, I began to make changes in my life. I moved out of my house, which was a residential Christian ministry, because I knew that being gay would eventually lead to me being kicked out, and I didn't want to cause such a fuss with my roommates. I started sharing who I really was with my friends and some of my family members. I didn't have a big "coming-out event," and I chose instead to do it on a case-by-case basis. My roommates for the most part were concerned, but they would still treat me well when I saw them in the future. The family members that I began to tell, such as my mother and brother, were accepting and loving. This love that I received truly helped me during that fragile time.

As I continued in school, I made it a point to explore a side of me that I had not had the chance to develop. I suppose I was fortunate enough to not have fallen into some of the traps that young gay men do when they first come out. I took things very slowly and focused on me rather than on finding someone else. I reconciled my religious beliefs with my sexuality and took the time to educate myself about what it really meant to be gay. I came out to more and more people and developed my true identity as a gay person. I began to discover that sexual orientation and morality were not correlates, and as I studied, I found examples of incredible people who also happened to be gay. My mind and thoughts broadened, and I began to feel good about myself again.

It was at this time that I decided to spend a year studying abroad. I soon found myself in the middle of Sweden and also in my first real relationship. I have to admit that I fell pretty hard, and although it ended when I came home a year later, it showed me that being gay is not just about sex, and love is just as important to our community as it is with anyone else. While I was in Sweden, I also met and became friends with students from all over the world. This insight into different cultures and perspectives reinforced my understanding that although someone is different, they should be treated as an individual and not as a race, religion, sex, or other characteristic. These life lessons would significantly shape my approach to being a cop later down the road.

After returning from Sweden, I began graduate school and completed two years toward a master's degree. During that time, I had a few boyfriends, but nothing too serious developed in my romantic life. My career in graduate school took up most of my time, and after a couple of years, I once again found myself in a position to make a big decision. I was having trouble in school, mostly due to the fact that after

I had taken many advanced courses in the area of my major—cognitive psychology—I began to realize that it did not capture my interest as I had anticipated it would. My grades began to suffer somewhat (keeping in mind that anything below an A is considered unsatisfactory), and the staff became concerned about my future in the department. My research was going along fine, but my performance in advanced inferential statistics fell below that ideal, and the decision was made to release me from the program just six months early of the completion of my master's degree. So, I left the university with an incomplete master's degree, a wealth of advanced knowledge, and no job.

At that point, I was in a bad place. I knew that although I didn't have too much debt, my student loans would come due soon, and I needed a source of income to take care of them. I began to search for a job in any place I could imagine. I tried newspapers, online searches, job services, and just about anywhere I saw a Now Hiring sign. I consistently worked on it for approximately three months, relying on my family in the interim to help me eat and pay bills. I then found a job listing that had promise; the Department of Corrections was continually hiring for parole officers, and they were about to test for a new group of employees. Although I had always been fascinated with law enforcement, up to that point, I had never actually considered a career in that field. The job made sense to me for a lot of practical reasons; it required a college degree (a nice thought that my years of work in school would not go to waste), it had pretty good job security, State benefits and retirement, and they would hire me quickly. The pay wasn't anything to get excited over, but it would help me get by while I tried to figure out where I was going in life. I looked at the opportunity as a detour from my original plans and possibly a stepping stone to "bigger and better" things. After a short period of consideration, I decided to put in an application. I was quickly contacted by the State and asked to take a test, which I made it through with very little effort. A short time later, I interviewed in Tulsa and was hired.

Again, here I was, looking at myself as someone I had never intended to be. This recurring theme in my life was becoming old hat by then, and I again chose to just rely on my faith and hope. I would really need it at this point because I moved to a city to take a job I had never imagined having, and I was living in an area I had never been to before.

I didn't know anyone, let along anyone in the gay community. But, as hope springs eternal, I jumped into my new life with optimism.

I can remember my first moment in the parole office with the other state officers. Not knowing exactly what to expect, I was just about floored at the reality of the job when I immediately heard a veteran officer chewing the rear clean off of a parolee in his office who had failed a drug test. The parolee was crying and sobbing, and the officer just sat there, stoic and angry, and he kept asking her if she was ready to go back to prison. Although experience would teach me that this approach is sometimes necessary in that line of work, it was a quick birth by fire for my first day as a law enforcement officer. I also met my first supervisor on that day, Ernie. Ernie was about six foot eight, and you could tell from talking to him that he had been doing the job for a very long time. Nothing a parolee could do would get past him, and he was a great teacher for my first few months dealing with convicted criminals. He taught me that my trust in people could be taken advantage of and that people would lie to me about their mistakes on a regular basis. This new understanding of the world was definitely at odds with my preference to trust those around me implicitly, and I had to learn how to see people for who they really are. It would take me much longer to understand that this "cop" sense did not necessarily mean that I had to lose my faith in people.

I met one of my best friends in life while in that office—Alice. She also hired on at the same time I did, and she was a beautiful younger lady who happened to be fluent in Spanish, something that could always come in handy in our line of work. As we began our training and went through the state's academy together, we became very good friends, and one night while we were out dancing at a local bar, I told her that I was gay. She laughed and stated that she had already figured it out, as most in the office had, and that nobody really cared. I was very relieved by what she said because I had for months tried to figure out whether I really wanted to come out on the job. Oklahoma affords no protection to gay people from discrimination in the workplace, and I knew that I could always be fired for being gay if the higher-ups decided to do it. It was always on my mind in the office, and I had kept a very low profile up to that point, mostly only talking shop to everyone I worked with. The knowledge that everyone already knew weighted heavily in my decision to be openly out at work, and for the two years that I would be in that office, it never seemed to cause a single problem for me.

While we were in the state academy, I had the pleasure of hearing a very enlightened instructor who had come to speak to the class about sex offender supervision. This woman worked at the prison in Oklahoma where sex offenders are housed (we have a separate facility for them in Oklahoma, mostly for their own safety). She began to teach about the psychology of sex offenders and predators, and then suddenly, out of the blue, she brought up the association that many believe to exist between sex offenders and homosexuals. She explained that there is no real correlation between the propensity to be a predator and a person's sexual orientation. This got some smirks from the class and even a few objections, but she kept to her guns and taught that that association was completely false and had been constructed to harm gay people by the homophobic political crowd. I was just amazed at her and that she felt it was important enough to bring this topic up during a more technical discussion of sex offender supervision. It was very inspiring for me because, for the first time, I had seen law enforcement as not necessarily being homophobic, a stereotype I had carried for most of my life.

After I had been a parole officer for two years, I started to become discontented. The job wasn't all that bad, having a regular shift and weekends off, but the pay was very low, and I was struggling month to month to survive. My student loans came due, and the payments were eating a huge percentage of my paycheck each month. I began looking for other positions, and without even realizing it, I was only looking for law enforcement jobs. I suppose by that time, I had settled in on the field, and my course in life had been permanently changed. I realized that I truly loved the job, especially the fieldwork where we went out to find and arrest an absconder. I was always the first to volunteer for prisoner transports or to arrest someone in the office, and I gravitated toward the "cop" aspects of the position. It was apparent that my detour into law enforcement had changed from a dirt bypass into a new highway in life. My upbringing and affinity for following the rules had given me the perfect foundation and mentality for being an officer, and when coupled with my broader understanding gained by being exposed to other cultures and perspectives, I found that getting out there to do what's right and help people straighten out was more rewarding than any other career field that I could have chosen for myself.

During my job search for a new position, something happened to me that would be the most important thing in my life. I met this guy Eddie online, and although we had not talked too much on the computer, we did begin calling each other, and he asked me out on a date on New Year's Eve. I thought I had to work and told him I couldn't, but then at the last minute, I was able to get out of the work, and I called him to ask if he still wanted to go out. He stated that he did, and he soon picked me up at my apartment. I immediately thought he was cute as hell, and I really enjoyed getting to know him at dinner. After eating, we went to Alice's annual New Year's party and ended up spending the night together. We were pretty much a couple after that first date, and within a few months we moved in together.

Eddie was a great boyfriend to have because he understood the whole "cop" thing about me. His father was a retired firefighter, and he knew the mind-set of knowing that your loved one is leaving to do a very dangerous job every day. We grew closer and closer, and one day, I came home to find him acting in a very strange manner. I couldn't put my finger on it, but I could tell that something was up. He asked if I wanted to take a bath to relax after work, and I told him that would be very nice. I sank into the tub and suddenly noticed a plastic duck floating in the water. Eddie was quirky like that, having an affinity for SpongeBob and other cartoons. I laughed and assumed that he was just being cute for me. As I picked up the duck, I noticed that there was a diamond ring on the tail. Now, people always tell me that I talk way too much and they wish that I had a roll of duct tape on my shoulder for their easy access. But, for the first time in my life, I was completely speechless. I picked up the ring and realized that it was a wedding ring that I had pointed out to him in a store window. I had told him that I really liked that style of ring and now I couldn't come up with what to say since he had bought it for me. I looked up at him, and he asked me to marry him. Every single nerve in my body went crazy at that moment, and I was dizzy, scared, in shock, and happier than I've ever been in life. I told him that I wanted him to be my family, and that afternoon I became engaged.

We decided that because we had such a short courtship, we would wait about two years to actually marry. In the meantime, I continued my search for a new job, and I put in an application for the Tulsa Police Department. I had worked with some officers from TPD and always found that they were professional, educated, and just nice people all the way around. It would have definitely been a good position for me, as the pay was considerably better, the benefits were competitive with the State's, and the job consisted of more of what I loved about law enforcement. I was called in for a physical agility test and to complete a background investigation. The physical test was no problem, but it took me several weeks to assemble the information for the background packet. I had to list every place I had ever lived, every job I had ever taken, and every speeding ticket I had ever received. When you move around as much as I did and live in as many places as I had, that is quite a feat. I also was unsure about whether or not I wanted to tell the hiring personnel that I was gay, but I would just cross that bridge when I came to it.

The academy informed me that I needed to schedule a board interview to continue with the process. I made my first appearance at the academy in my best suit and sat in front of the board not knowing what to expect. They asked me questions about how I would respond in certain situations and how I have dealt with problems in my jobs in the past. I walked out of the interview unsure if I was what they were looking for, but I remembered to have faith and hope that I had done well.

I was then taken into another office to interview with my background investigator. She was a formidable woman who was obviously, by the appearance of her office, very accustomed to giving maximum attention to detail. She began by flipping through the numerous pages of my background packet on her desk, and she asked me for clarification on a few items. We talked about why I wanted to be a cop and if I was aware of the risks that come along with it. I was comfortable knowing that I was going to be in possible danger every day when I came to work because I knew that what I would be doing was going to help others, and the benefits far outweighed the risks. At that point, all I could think about was that I wanted to be a cop and out in the field. Mentally and spiritually, I was ready.

My investigator then showed a wide grin on her face, and she stated,

"Now I'm going to get all up in your business. Who are you dating right now?" Well, needless to say, that question put me right into the fire. I had considered staying in the closet in this new job because I was not sure how an active police department would feel about an out gay man working with them. When she asked me this, however, the choice to come out or not shifted to whether or not I was going to truly be honest with her. Of course, I could have stated that I was single, because under the law, that was my official status. I could have questioned why she wanted to know that and whether it was relevant to the job. Or, I could just be honest and tell her that I was living and in a relationship with another man.

In the few seconds that I had to consider my options, a little voice in my head asked, "So, you want to dodge this? Why? If they are going to hire you, then they should hire you for who you really are. And, besides, you need to be honest; if you can't be honest about this, can you be honest enough to be an officer?" Well, the choice was clear to me after thinking of it that way.

"I'm actually in a relationship with my roommate," I heard myself say. My investigator then looked very confused, and she started flipping through the papers trying to figure out what I meant. She let out a quiet and long, "Oh," as she realized that I'm gay. She looked up at me, and I thought I'd be the first to speak and break up the uncomfortable moment. "Well, I wasn't sure whether it would be a problem for the department since the policies don't really address it." Again, a large grin came over her face, and she said, "Sir, the Tulsa Police Department is a professional organization. We do not practice discrimination on any level and this, of course, will not be a problem at all." I felt incredible relief when I heard her say that, and I was all at once more eager to get out there and be a cop. I also felt a little embarrassed that I had automatically assumed that the officers on the department would be homophobic, and they would not want to hire a gay person. I had stereotyped the department and had built up in my head the worst possible scenario without even considering giving these folks the chance to be comfortable with me. Needless to say, I had a lot on my mind when I left the interview.

A few weeks later, I received a call from my investigator asking me how the title "Tulsa Police Officer Thomas Bell" sounded. I told her that it sounded better than anything I had heard before. She told me that I would be expected to report to the academy in a few months and to be ready. Although I knew that I had to begin getting into shape and I also needed to get into the studying mind-set, I also had to consider how "out" I wanted to be in the academy. I knew that the staff and current officers would know that I was gay, but I had no idea if the other cadets would have a clue.

We started the class in the middle of the summer, and after a few days, I figured out that the staff did not out me to my classmates. I kept a low profile for the first couple of weeks to get a feel for the class. It was a stress-induced environment with plenty of pushups, yelling, and drills. I hadn't thought too much about coming out during the first few weeks because I was too busy trying to catch my own ass and keep up. After I discovered that the class would share locker rooms and showers after workouts, I made the tactical decision to not come out to my class until after graduation. While I did feel a little hypocritical for doing this, I thought that the level of stress we were being put under for the training would not be helped if some of my classmates freaked out because they were changing clothes in front of a gay person. I never actually felt compelled to remain in the closet by any staff or department officials, but I simply wanted to concentrate on my studying and didn't want to make too many waves in the already choppy seas of our academy experience.

Six months, a million pushups, thousands of spent rounds, and one crushed kneecap later, I put on my official police uniform and drove to the academy in the wee hours of the morning. I met my classmates there—a group who I had grown to love and respect and I had come to understand as my second family. Later that morning, I raised my hand along with the other cadets, and I swore to uphold the law, to protect and serve, and to give my life if need be. My chief handed me my badge, and my mother pinned it on my chest. This was one of the proudest moments of my life, first, because I had become a police officer, and second, because I had become a police officer for a department who knowingly and happily hired an out gay man to work for them.

Field training was next, and this would be my first exposure to the department as a whole. I reported a couple of months later (after a brief detour for knee surgery) and began to take calls with my field training officer. It didn't take long before I realized that pretty much everyone out there had found out that there was a gay officer from the newest academy class, and many were at least intrigued to meet me. The weeks of training went by pretty quickly, and it wasn't until the last part that I encountered negativity for being gay. I was in the computer room at one of the divisions at the end of a shift and was working on paperwork when several officers came into the room. They were talking to each other, and one of them suddenly started talking in a lispy voice to the others. He continued doing so in spite of the fact that I didn't bother to even glance at him.

After a while, I left the room to turn in my paperwork, and one of the officers followed me out. She pulled me aside and apologized for the way he was trying to make fun of me, and she reassured me that he did not speak for the other officers. I was impressed and touched that she would do this because she wasn't involved in it, and she had no obligation to say anything, but nonetheless she went out on a limb to make sure that I felt welcomed and comfortable at that division. I thanked her and told her that I really didn't care that he was making fun of me. After all, he didn't even know anything about me, and I wasn't about to waste my time trying to correct his unfortunate attitude. I would again run into him several times throughout the next few years, and he never failed to suddenly start talking with a lisp when I was within earshot. To this day, I have never bothered to dignify his immaturity with a response.

I soon finished field training and was finally assigned to a permanent position on day shift. Again, I felt uneasy because I would now interact directly with my new squad mates, and this time without the protection of a field training officer. The squad that I was assigned to was made up of some of the most veteran officers on the department (lovingly known as Jurassic Squad). Although I could be certain that they knew I was gay before I went to my first meeting, I was unsure if I would be accepted as all the other new officers had been. I quickly realized that my skepticism lost out to my faith again, and I fit right in with this bunch. It was a great opportunity for a new officer like me because these cops had an arsenal of field experience that I could learn from, and I was right at home before too long. While I didn't really speak too openly about my sexuality, I also never once felt that these veteran officers, who undoubtedly came from a law enforcement background that was not too tolerant of gay people, treated me any differently because I was gay. They always welcomed me as one of the squad and included me in everything that was going on.

The job was not the only thing good going on in my life at that time. Shortly after I was "cut loose" in the field, I stood next to Eddie in front of our families, friends, and even some officers I worked with, and vowed to spend the rest of my life with him. Our wedding was held at our home, and we did the whole thing ourselves with the help of our friends. My brother was my best man, and Alice walked in with him. Eddie also had a best "man," Kim, and our good friend Amanda was the flower girl (at eighteen, she was happy to finally have the opportunity to be one, something she had always dreamed about). It was the happiest moment of my life. I somehow felt that all of the faith and hope I had kept was being rewarded, and for the first time in my life, I felt true peace in my heart. I was so happy and excited that when I said my vows, I kissed Eddie to seal the deal, having forgotten to give him his ring first.

As a now married gay man, I continued working in the field, and I discovered that there is no other job on the planet I would rather do than being a cop. It is the one job where you can see the best and worst things possible within the span of a few hours. I especially love the times when I have the opportunity to really help people and to see their lives get better because we're out there. I found that faith and hope are universal, whether being used to hold your family together through a tragedy or to lift yourself up to be a better person.

On one day that I'll remember for a long time, I was at a division when I ran into a woman who I worked with regularly. I had just recently changed my last name so that Eddie and I would have the same, and I was filing about a million memos to notify everybody of the change. As I was at the desk making copies, this officer looked at me and said, "You know, I just want you to know how much I admire you for being who you are and not being apologetic about it. I think it's really cool that you changed your name and you're not ashamed of it." There have been very few times that I have been that proud to be on my department, and on that day, she truly reminded me that I was part of a family. I have also had numerous wonderful experiences with both fellow officers and supervisors, and they regularly ask about Eddie and are interested in what's going on in my life.

At this point in my career, I guess you could say that I'm completely "out" on the department. The funny thing is, though, that my orientation rarely—if ever—comes up. I have recently been assigned to a specialty position that carries a significant amount of responsibility, and this is a sign to me that the leadership of the department has faith in me and my abilities, regardless of my sexual orientation. When I work with my fellow officers, they always treat me like anyone else; I am always part of the ongoing jabs and jokes, they support me whenever I need something, and I'm included in the activities that go on around me.

It might be somewhat surprising to many to know that a police department in the very conservative state of Oklahoma would be so comfortable with an openly gay officer, and I realize that this is certainly not the norm. But I can't help but believe that perhaps the one reason that being gay hasn't been a problem for me is because I am comfortable with myself, and that self-confidence is something that people recognize and respond to. I'm out there for everyone to see; I have nothing to hide or be evasive about, and I have no problems talking to others about my sexuality if the topic comes up. Cops by nature tend to be skeptical, and showing them that I'm completely honest with them disarms the usual feeling of distrust and misunderstanding.

The one most important thing I have learned on this journey of becoming who I am today is to always have faith and hope, especially when dealing with people. I have heard that if you are expected to be a certain way all the time and you are faced with this expectation for a long enough period, then eventually you will become that way. To me, this means that if I expect people to be prejudiced all the time, perhaps their response to me being gay is due in part to the fact that I never gave them a chance to be okay with me. The officers on my department have consistently surprised me, from the day I first interviewed to the day I introduced Eddie to them as my spouse and to the day that I decided to pen my story for this book. I now know that if I am willing to be the first one to extend a friendly hand, the vast majority of my fellow officers will respond in kind. In giving them the chance to not be discriminatory, I am showing them the same respect and consideration that I hope to receive from them in spite of my orientation.

If you are an officer who is considering coming out on your department, or if you are a gay person who wants to become a police officer, the best advice I can give you is to give people a chance. This job requires an incredible spirit, and one thing that is paramount to doing it well is to trust wholeheartedly in those who have your back. We put one another's lives in our hands every day, and the feeling of family between us is something that very few will ever understand. I know that, without any doubt, I would take a bullet for any other officer on this department, regardless of who they are or whether or not they are homophobic. The crazy thing is, though, that I know that even the homophobic officers would do the same for me anytime. That is who we are. As they say, blood is always thicker than water, especially when that blood is blue.

# BRETT DUNCKEL

One night while enjoying a rare moment of relaxation in front of the television at Fire Station 66, my department would change forever. On this particular shift, we had an overtime person for twenty-four hours. As his penance for invading our station, he was forced to buy dessert. Being the health-conscious crew we were, we selected flavored popsicles.

As we sat enjoying some television program we could all only half agree upon, I noticed my female co-worker sitting beside me. She, of course, was eating one of the popsicles just like the rest of us. When she saw me looking at her, she pretended to give the popsicle a blowjob. Hey, it's a fire station—we do weird things! She then proceeded to jokingly ask me if she was doing it right. Well, at that moment, it became clear to me it was time to reveal my true self. I turned to her and said," You're doing it all wrong. Let me show you how it's really done!" So, I proceeded to show her my skills!

Well, it suddenly became clear to the rest of the guys sitting on either side of us what was going on. Once the initial shock over what they had just witnessed wore off, the room burst into one of the loudest fits of laughter I have ever been witness to. The guy to my left actually fell out of his recliner because he was laughing so hard.

And thus began a new chapter not only in my career, but in my life.

Flashing back to November 8, 1999, I still get a huge sense of pride as I remember walking into the small conference room of Fire Station 4. Neatly laid out on the conference table in front of us were nine brand-new helmets, each complete with its new owner's last name blazoned across the back. Alongside the helmets was an assortment of smaller pieces of gear—flashlight, Leatherman, fanny pack filled with miscellaneous medical gear, and a few other items we would need as firefighters. It had finally hit me; I was now truly a firefighter.

This journey first began for me when I was a young child. I was home playing in my bedroom when I noticed the distinct odor of smoke. I immediately ran and told my parents and brothers, who then joined me to investigate the source of the smell. Once we stepped out of our front door and looked down the street, we immediately saw the source. Our neighbor's house, a mere two doors down, was billowing thick, black smoke. As I looked on in absolute horror, I saw various firefighters running through the thick smoke into the house. Clear as day, I still remember thinking to myself, *Who in their right mind would ever want to do that?*

Years later, as I began high school, some friends of mine from the swim team told me about a program they had joined called Fire Explorers. They explained to me that it was basically junior firefighters. They went to weekly meetings and learned about firefighting and first aid. I decided that it sounded exciting and that I would go with them to one of these meetings. Well, I found it interesting enough to return for a second and then a third meeting, and by the end of the month, I was a full probationary member. Once I got enough training, I was allowed to do ride-alongs, and that's when I became hooked.

At around this same time, there was a lot of confusion and conflict running through my head. I guess I could have been labeled the typical high school freshman trying to navigate the daily mix of classes, lunchtime, social groups, and the occasional bully. I was lucky in that I knew some of the upperclassmen from my time spent in the pool as a year-round, competitive swimmer. For three hours a day, five days a week, I swam with them, scantily clad in a Speedo. They tended to look out for me.

My difficulty in high school wasn't due to the typical hardships faced in school. My struggle was completely internal, and I knew it had to remain so. I was acutely aware that I would be in for some hard times had this struggle become public knowledge. I did not understand it one bit, and I was the one going through it. How in the world, then, would my friends and classmates even slightly understand? So I continued with my internal struggle, carefully hidden away from everyone.

I knew I liked to look at guys in swim practice and at school. I knew I had this odd attraction that I could not explain. I wanted to be with these guys I fancied all the time. I wanted to be close to them, to hold them. It was in stark conflict to the way I was told things worked, yet it seemed to me to be the only way things should work. I could not understand why the other guys didn't feel the same way I did. Why was it that they seemed to have these same feelings, yet their feelings were directed toward girls? I could look at the girls in school and know which were good-looking, yet I did not have any of the same desires toward these girls that my friends had.

I felt so isolated for having these thoughts. I couldn't imagine another guy my age feeling the same way. This ate at me. It was something that I would think about constantly. Even though I had heard a few things about gay people and even saw a few examples in the media, I did not associate myself with being gay in any way. I was an athlete, macho, I was in the fire explorer program with hopes of becoming a firefighter after graduation; these things were in total conflict with what I knew of a gay person. I told myself that I could not be gay.

After some time, my feelings toward guys only grew stronger. I still could look at a girl and know when she was attractive, but I did not have any desire to be with one sexually or to date one. More and more of my friends were dating and going to parties, yet I avoided both as best I could. I wanted to be like them, yet I knew it would only be a lie. These were very difficult feelings I was having, and the fact that I knew I had to keep them secret made it all the worse. I felt as though if the truth were reveled, I would be a huge disappointment to all of those in my life. I figured that I would lose all of my friends and family. It was killing me that I had no one to talk to about my feelings, and I did not know if anyone else even had these same feelings.

Graduation came and went. I never did date anyone in high school and never really did go to any parties. Luckily for me, nobody ever really pushed either issue. I was now ready to put all of my focus and energy into becoming a firefighter. I figured that by doing so, I could forget these feelings, or somehow they would change.

The fire academy was pretty uneventful. I loved it and hated it, as I'm sure most do. I would always avoid looking south in the locker room or shower, even though there were a few guys I was definitely fond of. I avoided conversations about girlfriends and dating. Once class was over, I would go home and not associate with my classmates outside of class. After class on Fridays, everyone would go to one of the local bars and hang out; I, instead, would get in my car and go home. I occasionally look back on that time and realize how much I missed out on.

During the fire academy, I discovered that even though I was very quiet, I kind of had an ability to fit in with most any of the cliques. I could be found with the group of guys who picked up Horshack's car and placed it in the middle of the parking spaces between the parking stones. To this day, I don't know how he got it out! Yet I could also fit right in talking to the same guy about his family. In some senses, I feel my internal struggle had helped give me this ability to fit in so well.

Once I was finished with the fire academy and EMT school, it was time to find a job. Now to those of you unfamiliar with full-time, paid fire department jobs, they are very difficult to get. Through the explorer program, I had made a lot of contacts that I hoped would help me in my job search. At around this same time, the Internet was starting to become more widespread. Once we became an Internet-equipped household, I started to do a little research on these feelings I had.

I came across a site known as Oasis. On this site, kids and young adults who were in similar situations as I was, as well as those more open about themselves, would write stories to share with their readers. These stories had a range of topics, yet they all related to the author's sexuality. Looking back, I guess you could consider this the prequel to the modern blog. This was the first time I found guys who felt the same way I did. Well, I read every article I could find on this site. I also started to e-mail some of the authors on the site and ask them questions I could never find the right person to ask. This helped me tremendously, yet I still had a hard time identifying as gay. It was at this time that I decided that I wanted to help others who also felt like I did and thus began my outreach as "Tyler." At the time, I was still hiding my true self from everyone, hence the pen name.

I was afraid to use my real name, as I thought someone would be able to search me out and discover my secret. As Tyler, I could freely talk about my situation with a reasonable assurance that I was safe. I began to tell my story up to that point. I began receiving e-mails from kids all over the country. I heard all sorts of stories and got all kinds of questions. I did my best to help these kids as the other authors had helped me. I even ended up meeting a college kid who wanted to become a police officer after graduation. We began an online friendship and later met in person. We remain friends to this day. He currently works as a full-time police officer; however, he has not made the step to come out in his department yet.

During this time of my life, I one day woke up and had an epiphany. It was as though someone had flipped on a light switch in my brain, and a giant neon rainbow-colored sign glowed to life, saying, "I'm gay!" Once that sign was finally turned on, it seemed to all become so clear. I felt as though I finally had an identity. The problem was that I still did not fit any of the stereotypes I mistakenly knew of gay people. I think that is why it took me so long to admit to myself that I was gay and not bisexual, which was a label I toyed with for awhile. It wasn't until I started meeting other gay guys who I found to be "normal" like me that I fully embraced the fact that I was gay.

I then began the task of looking for local gay guys who loosely fit into the group with which I identified—straight-acting guys who liked guys! Of course I now know that I was a bit misguided at the time, but hey, I was a newbie. I found a couple of guys who I would become friends with over time. Eventually, I found one who was in the ROTC program at Texas A&M and who was going through a lot of the same things that I was. He had ambitions of a career in law enforcement yet was concerned about his sexuality. He became my closest gay friend and is to this day one of my most important friends. He later got hired with a very good department and has not only come out on the job but has become his department's GLBT liaison and a member of their SWAT team!

Shortly before meeting him, I finally got a job offer with the department I am currently with. I was so excited and yet so worried. That was it; I was now a full-fledged firefighter. The excitement was mixed because I was hiding this huge secret that I did not think would go over well at all in the fire service. I still had not even told any of my family or friends. I figured that if my secret got out at the fire department, I would be ridiculed and possibly face physical harm. I was more concerned with the effects coming out would have on my work environment than I was with my family and friends finding out. So, at work, I went even deeper in the closet. However, I told myself that I did not want to lie to anyone. For some reason, I felt that being a liar was worse than being found out as gay. I guess I would not do well as a politician.

So how did I stay in the closet in one of the most macho, homophobic careers out there, yet never tell the lie that I was straight? Well, that was not always an easy task. It became necessary for me to become a witty, quick thinker. During the first few months on the job as I met and worked with different people each shift, everyone would inevitably ask about my girlfriend, wife, kids, family, and so on. You quickly find out, being in such close proximity during a twenty-four-hour shift with the same group of people, that just about every topic eventually comes up. For that twenty-four-hour period, there is no escaping, and it is difficult hiding your true likes and dislikes. In the beginning, it was easy to tell everyone that I was single and just concentrating on making it though my first year as a probationary firefighter. They seemed to buy it.

So I survived my first year and was no longer a probationary firefighter. Now what? Well, I had to go to paramedic school, of course—one year of hell which allowed my cover to be extended. So as I settled into a routine with my second-year team, we rotated stations each month yet remained with the same team of people. Some of them become curious about my lack of a girlfriend and silence on the topic of my life outside of the fire department. My silence was not from a lack of a life, but rather from a lack of a life that could be shared with them. So now, my paramedic school excuse seemed to be less convincing. I needed to come up with a little something more. When asked about a girlfriend or going out that weekend, I would usually just tell them that I went out with friends, which was not a lie, just a half truth. After some time, I started to get some guys who would joke that I was gay and even ask if I was gay or ask if I was out with the boys over the weekend. Now, when they would do this, it was in a joking manner, but I definitely knew the suspicions were running wild. I knew that my time in the closet was becoming shorter and shorter.

This caused me to have to think fast so as not to lie and yet to remain in the closet. So I would turn it around on them. "Why are you asking me? Are you trying to get a date? Why do you care? Is there something you're not telling us?" Usually, this worked like a charm. There is nothing better for stopping a guy from inquiring about your sexuality than using his own homophobia against him and calling his sexuality into question.

At this same time, I was having serious thoughts of leaving the fire service altogether. I was very concerned with what would happen if I were ever "outed" in the department. I didn't think I would be accepted, and I thought that I would be ridiculed every day. The fear you feel as a closeted individual in this type of profession can be extremely overwhelming. I figured that since I was a paramedic, I could transition into a registered nursing program while still remaining at the fire department. Then, once I became an RN, I could quit the department and support myself while figuring out my next career path. However, I told myself that I would not leave the department for at least a year in order to be absolutely sure that it was the right decision to make. Well, I'm sure you've figured out by now that my decision was to stay in the fire service.

While this struggle to stay in the closet at work was going on, I had yet another epiphany. I had watched a Showtime movie called *Common Ground*, which was comprised of three short films. Each one touched upon a different story related to a gay person's struggle with homophobia. The one that really touched me was the one starring Jonathan Taylor Thomas from *Home Improvement*. He played a high school student who happened to be on the swim team and was struggling with being gay. He finds solace in his gay French teacher. There is a scene in which he is telling his teacher that he just wants to know what it is like to be able to hold a guy and feel that comfort. That really hit home with me. It was at that point when I felt that it was time to come out of the closet to my family.

So how did I come out to my family? There were so many things that I wanted to tell them to help them understand, yet I knew I would not have the emotional strength to get through everything without breaking down. A letter seemed to be the best way to get everything out; however, it seemed so impersonal. Well, explanation won out over being impersonal. I sat down at my computer and began to type my three-page coming-out letter. I was a wreck. I knew that once it was finalized, my family would never see me the same way again. I feared I would forever become known as the gay one in the family. I didn't want that to become the one thing that defined me as a person. So as I spilled my internal struggle onto paper, I tried to reiterate to them that nothing about me had changed. I still liked doing the same things, still enjoyed the same music, and still put my shoes on one foot at a time. The only difference was that they now knew everything about me. I no longer had to hide this hugely important part of me.

I decided that I would leave the letter for them to read while I was on shift. That was the longest twenty-four hours of my life. A million thoughts ran through my head. Fear, confusion, regret, you name it. I kept checking my cell phone between calls to see if they had tried to reach me. Nothing. Finally, 0700 rolled around, and I packed my gear into my locker and got into my car for that long drive home. At this time, I had not moved out yet, so when I got home, I expected them to be waiting for me. I didn't know if they would be standing in the front lawn with all my belongings packed in boxes ready for me to move out or if I would be greeted with tears and understanding. Well, when I walked in, I was greeted with nothing. They were in their room getting ready for work, as usual. So I went to my room and set about my usual routine. After awhile, my dad walked into my room and stood in the doorway. The first thing he said to me was, "That must have been the hardest letter for you to write." Of course, once he said that, I had tears streaming down my face. He followed that by saying that no matter what, he and my mother still loved me and would always love me. Once that big step was taken, I searched out a few books for them to read to help them better understand homosexuality. I also had a conversation with my mom one day which I think finally helped her understand it a bit more. One day, while riding in the car with her, I told her that she didn't choose to fall in love with my father; it just happened. She had no control over those feelings. For me, it is the same way. I have no control over who I'm attracted to; it's just something that happens. It's just the way my brain was wired. When she thought of it that way, it seemed to make a lot more sense.

My coming out to my friends was kind of a funny situation. My mother had been asking me if I had come out to any of friends yet and how I was planning on doing it. I told her that I did not want to do it until I had told my brothers. Well, telling them was pretty uneventful. I basically sent them a shortened version of the letter that I gave to my parents. Neither of them had any problem with it.

A lot of my friends are also friends with my middle brother. We were only a grade apart, and both of us were on the swim team together, so we had a lot of friends in common. One evening, we were downtown at an event called Christmas on Las Olas—basically a holiday street festival. One of our friends was a boat captain on a local charter boat. After his charter was done for the evening, a bunch of us met up on his boat to have drinks. Once we all had our drinks in hand, the group turned toward me, and I immediately knew it was over! The spokesman of the group asked the question, to which I answered, "Yep!" His next question was why it took so long for me to tell them. He was actually a little bit hurt that I didn't think I could tell him or any of our other friends. Once I explained the tremendous fear that goes along with this secret, he quickly understood.

So now that I was out to family and friends, I was slowly gaining confidence as a gay male. I was making gay friends and even going on a few dates. I spared my straight friends most details of my gay life. However, I did let them know that I would answer any questions they had. And they sure did ask questions!

Once I had built up more confidence, I started to think of my coming out in the fire service. How would I do it? What reactions would I get? Would it bring about any negatives? Should I even do it to begin with? Well, the last question was quickly answered by virtue of the toll it was taking on me having to hide everything from my co-workers. Every time I was out, I would always be looking over my shoulder to make sure nobody from work saw me with any of my gay friends. It was driving me crazy! The time had come.

So after that fateful evening at Station 66 eating popsicles and watching television, I was out in the fire department. Of course, it wasn't like everyone instantly knew; word had to spread. As a lot of you know, in police and fire departments, word spreads like wildfire. For the next few weeks, people would come up to me and ask if the rumors were true, to which I would reply, "Yes, they are!" For the most part, I was met with a great bit of admiration. People would tell me how much courage it must have taken to come out. A lot of them had questions but were afraid or embarrassed to ask, so I made it a point to let everyone know that if they had the courage to ask me a question, no matter the topic, I would answer their question. There were, of course, a few people who were uncomfortable at first, but once they realized that I was the exact same person as before, they became more at ease around me.

I remember one evening at the station; we were all ready for bed. The station I was at this particular shift happened to be a temporary trailer while our new station was being built, so most of us were in one large bunkroom. Once the lights went out, one of the guys asked me a goofy question related to me being gay. One of my co-workers stepped in and told him that it was probably not right for him to ask me that question. I then made it a point to let them all know that I would answer any questions they asked. Boy, did the question floodgates open! For the next two hours or so, we all laid in our beds with the lights out having a question-and-answer session about homosexuality and bisexuality. It was quite entertaining, and I feel it also helped those guys gain an understanding of being gay which they would probably never have gotten had I not had the courage to step out of the closet.

Another story I find very entertaining happened one afternoon when I ventured downstairs from my office to the station. The building which houses our administrative offices is a three-story building with the fire station taking up the first floor, administrative offices the second, and training and the emergency operations center the third. I currently work in administration as a fire prevention captain, so I no longer work a twenty-four-hour shift. However, I frequently visit the stations to hang out with the shift personnel with whom I worked for a number of years.

On this particular day, the crew who was on shift was largely guys I had worked with extensively when I was on shift. We did a lot of joking around before and after I came out, and the joking continues to this day. When I walked into the kitchen, I noticed my name on the dry erase board. Next to my name was the name of a co-worker's fiancée. This co-worker happened to be someone I refer to as my work husband. He is someone I am attracted to and would date if it were not for the fact he is heterosexual and engaged. They had drawn a line between his fiancée's name and mine, creating a scoreboard. Under my name were approximately eighteen hash marks, and under her name were three and a half. I had no idea what this meant, so I asked one of the guys in the kitchen. He started laughing and began to tell me how this scoreboard was created during breakfast. This co-worker normally is not on this shift but was filling in for someone on this day. During breakfast, the topic of his upcoming marriage was brought up. At one point, some of the guys began to tell this co-worker that he should not get married. This was done jokingly but with a small amount of truth due to the high divorce rate some of my co-workers seem to have. Someone then spoke up and told him that he should consider breaking up with his fiancée to start dating me! This quickly got some of the guys to start coming up with reasons why I would make a better mate than his fiancée. The scoreboard was then created to keep an accurate count so my co-worker would be convinced of which potential mate would be best.

I, of course, started laughing at the thought of this conversation occurring. I then came up with a few of my own reasons I felt he should do as they suggested. This surprised the few guys who were standing with me, because they had not thought of those same reasons. My number then grew even larger! Well, none of this seemed to persuade the co-worker it was intended to because he went on to get married. Oh well—it still made for a very comical breakfast for the guys.

Coming out in my department has been best thing I could have ever done. It has helped me tremendously both in the department and even more in my personal life. I am no longer afraid to be seen in public by someone I work with. I have now made a tremendous number of close friends at work that I regularly associate with outside of work. By coming out in my fire department, I have had the opportunity to break any stereotypes that my fellow firefighters may have had. In doing so, not only have I changed their minds, but I have been able to change the minds of their families, as well. As a young gay person in this country, I know we must do everything we can to gain every ally we can. Equal rights will not just be given to us; we must fight for them. The more minds we can change about what and who we really are, the more of these allies we will gain in our fight for equal rights.

If you are struggling in your department because of your sexuality, stop letting it ruin your career and possibly your life. If there is one thing I have learned in my job as a firefighter, it is that life is so fragile and can be taken in the blink of an eye. It wasn't until after I came out that I realized the toll being in the closet was taking on me. I know that not everyone will have the same positive experience that I had, but I can assure you that no matter how difficult a time you may have, it is nothing compared to the pain and suffering you will have staying in the closet. Know that you are far from alone in your struggle. There are so many more gay and lesbian firefighters and police officers in the closet than we will ever know. The only way for us to make being gay or lesbian as commonplace as your eye color is for us all to come out of the closet and show everyone that we are just like them. We are just as good at our jobs as they are. We go through the same struggles they do. No matter what negativity we may face, we are not going anywhere.

Brett Dunckel
Fire Prevention Captain
Deerfield Beach Fire Rescue
ffdunk@gmail.com

# ALEX MORFIN

I have been a police officer for five years. About two years ago, I came out to the officers I was working with. Most of the officers were supportive and didn't care about my sexual orientation. These officers, who are still my friends, knew being gay did not interfere with my ability to perform my job. However, a few select officers made my job difficult. Name all the clichés, they happened. I was made fun of, ridiculed behind my back, denied backup on violent calls for service, and finally terminated. I was terminated less than thirty days after telling my chief that I was homosexual.

I was full of rage when I was terminated. Well, officially, I was asked to resign. I asked the chief why, and he did not have an answer for me. I informed him that I would not resign and was therefore terminated by force. I was told by officers who were still my friends that the chief had my uniforms burned after I turned them in. He gave my uniforms to the public works department and told them to "burn that fag's stuff."

I began the process of suing the department. In the middle of this grueling process, I asked myself if I still wanted to be a police officer. The answer was yes. I decided whether I won or lost a lawsuit, I would never be a police officer again. I settled with the police department and cut my losses.

Another police department hired me about three months after the last one terminated me. I fought with myself trying to figure out if I should come out or stay in the closet at this new department. I knew if I were fired again, I would not be able to handle it. I waited a year before I said anything to anybody and then slowly came out. Thankfully, my decision to come out again did not backfire on me. I have recently been promoted to detective and am very happy.

With as much hatred as I have for my old chief, if I saw him, I would have to thank him. He taught me a valuable lesson about people in law enforcement. Also, his firing me was the best thing that could have happened to my career. Luckily, it worked out for me. I know a lot of officers have not been as lucky as I have. That's why I wanted to share my story. Not for me, but for the officers who have been discriminated against in the past, present, and unfortunately, the ones who will be discriminated against in the future.

# JESSICA McGUINNESS

From a posting on my Facebook page to my co-workers:

> I'm not exactly sure how to start this off because the
> moment I click "Post," a big part of my life is going to
> change. I'm going to try to keep this post as short as
> I can, but no promises. As I'm sure most of you have
> heard, there are several rumors going around about me.
> In light of some recent events and comments, I decided
> that the personal details of my life will not be told by
> convenience store clerks and hospital dispatchers. This
> new Facebook group gave me the opportunity to tell
> my story in my own words to the select people without
> being interrupted or losing my chain of thought. At
> the very least, I hope to educate the people of our EMS
> agency on a subject that not many understand. And
> after going through this process for the past four years,
> I'm prepared to open Pandora's box. That being said, I
> will begin.

I'm going to begin this paragraph by just coming out and saying it. I am transgendered and have been going through the long, hard process of changing my life for the past four years. Wow, I said it! So now that we got that out of the way, allow me to give some background on my situation. I remember feeling different as early as the age of five. I had a clue about what it was, but I was too young to put my finger on it. I remember starting school and being rejected by the girls, and the boys made fun of me for trying to play with the girls. Around this time, I remember my marine brother casually using the word "fag." So at the earliest points of my life, I learned that there was something wrong with me, and I had to ignore it; otherwise, people would hate me.

In the early to mid-1980s, I remember watching talk shows like Morton Downey Jr., Sally Jesse Raphael, and Geraldo. On these shows, I remember how poorly the trans community was treated, and I thought, *Oh, please, God, I can't be like them. Please make this go away.* So I pushed it deeper and deeper. Living "gender dysphoric" was the hardest thing to deal with in my life.

As the years went on, I repressed this side of me very well, and it stayed my "dirty little secret." I always found masculine things, such as hockey and my family love for the Marine Corps. I had to hold on to these types of things in hopes that it would help beat this thing out of me. I also became very quiet and shy because I don't believe I ever really knew who I was or where exactly I fit in. I think my late teens and early twenties were the easiest time I had repressing it. Why? Because I was a pothead, acidhead, drunken idiot. Looking back, I realized that I was hiding from something dark in my life, and the drugs and alcohol gave me something different to focus on. When I was twenty-two, I stopped the drugs but continued to drink. Now, I wasn't drinking all the time. I used to focus on my jobs, and they always came first. Besides, that gave me something else to focus on instead of my problem. But when it was my days off, look out! It wasn't until my late twenties when this problem hit me again, *hard*, and this was the darkest time of my life. Most of you didn't see this, but I was a total mess. I would drink alone in my apartment and randomly break things. I remember feeling so much stress but not knowing where it was coming from. I'm not too bright, and I wasn't realizing that this was from thirty years of repressing who I am until one fateful summer night in West Virginia changed all that.

I always said that falling off that bridge was the best thing that ever happened to me. Now let me explain why. In the many months of recovery, I was unable to move from my couch. This gave me a lot of time to think about things. I thought about if I had died that night, I would have never reached my full potential. I was terrified about the thought of coming out to friends, family, and co-workers. Totally breaking down thirty years of my life and rebuilding it from scraps was not going to be easy. I just kept thinking about how those poor people were treated on those talk shows and saw myself on that stage. I came up with a three-year plan. I knew that I needed to get out of emergency medical services. As all of you know, public safety is not too GLBT friendly. I decided to spend my first year coming out to friends and family and going to therapy. I then would enter the two-year program at beauty school, and hopefully by then, I would have been on hormone replacement for a year when I graduated. I would then leave work and simply be able to switch roles by finding a new job. I was hoping to be out of the EMS agency and living in a new part of the city before everyone learned about me, and I wouldn't have to deal with the remarks from co-workers. I hoped that the changes to my body from the hormones would be so gradual that co-workers wouldn't notice, and the only telltale sign would be growing my hair out. I researched the hair policy and decided to act like a rebel. But in reality, I wanted to keep my wallflower status more than ever.

To say that the next few years were extremely stressful is an understatement. Coming out to friends and family was hard. I lost several childhood friends, and my family was very confused. I became the new hot conversation topic for the people that I was closest to. Eventually, this became old news, and most of my family showed me more love than anyone could imagine. The jury is still out on several of my family members, but I hope it won't be a big deal as time goes on.

Now let me tell about my life when school started. I was working my normal midnight shift along with being at school Monday through Thursday. This made for a sixty- to seventy-hour workweek. On top of that, Tuesday mornings were dedicated to four different doctors because I'm the first transgendered hemophiliac in the world, and my doctors didn't know what to expect. My conditions lead to many blood tests, MRIs, and mental evaluations. Wednesday mornings were for therapy and required support groups. Some of these appointments required me to go in "girl mode," but some didn't, so sometimes I had to go to one appointment in the morning and then come home and shower so I could go to the afternoon appointment in "boy mode."

My entire life was upside down. I was still dealing with the coming-out process, and then I had to hide it when I came into work. So please take a minute to think about how my schedule was for two years. Every day, I was on the go from the early morning until late at night. Sadly, my biggest casualty was my dog Bungi. Giving him up killed me, but I couldn't take care of him, and it was better for him. When I would come into work, the comments about my hair didn't seem to be a big deal, but considering the stress I was under, every little bit was huge to me. I had to stick with my story because my entire life was so unstable; I needed the stability of the EMS agency. Besides, without this job, I couldn't continue with my plan. The thing that got me through this period was telling myself, "It's only temporary, Jess. Think about the finish line." In order to help me deal with the stress at the EMS agency, I did tell a few co-workers so I could vent from time to time. This is also how all the rumors got back to me. These co-workers will remain nameless.

By the time I finished school in June of 2008, all the therapy was over. Before being discharged, my therapist said that I am one of the most well-put-together people she ever worked with. The doctors had what they needed, and those visits stopped, too. My friends and family were completely accepting. I have been on hormones since March of 2007.

After two years of the hardest work I ever did, I was back down to a forty-hour workweek (whew). My plan was hard, but it had worked perfectly. Coming out was over, and I decided to take a break and enjoy all of my hard work. I was going to use this time to enjoy how I have blossomed. This started the best period of my life. For the first time in my entire life, I loved what I saw in the mirror. After thirty years of agony, I found complete inner peace. I began to get very good at my new role and completely relished it. At this point, my family and friends have not seen the boy "Jesse" for two years. Everyone began to accept that Jesse did die under that bridge, and they learned to love Jessica. Everyone around me sees how happy and bubbly I am now. The person that was once so quiet won't shut up now. And believe it or not, I'm actually not bad looking.

The only problem during this period was that I had to rip down who I was every week I go to work. Then the economy broke down, and I was stuck working there because no salons were hiring.

This brings me to today. I've heard a lot of anti-transgender slander coming from my co-workers. I've heard a lot of dehumanizing terms, such as calling them *freaks*, *it*, or *he/she*. I have also personally witnessed people getting treated like a circus sideshow while in the emergency room. Once, a fellow co-worker walked around the ER and told the entire staff to go into the room and look at "it." Meanwhile, all I saw was a woman who just wanted to be left alone with her sick mother. More recently, I had to stand around and listen to co-workers discuss transgender issues while standing in the garage. Some of it included a co-worker calling a supervisor to a scene simply to laugh at the transgendered "freak" because of how "disgusting it was." Actually, this co-worker refused to call her anything but the most dehumanizing term, *it*. Another co-worker said that there should be no surgeries for trans-people because "Wearing a dress is one thing, but who would want to cut it off?" To me, this person was implying that only a sick person would ever want to do such a thing. I stood there and took everything in that was being said. I'm ashamed of myself that I said nothing to fire back.

These are the reasons why I never wanted to come out at work, and this type of ignorance is the reason that I repressed who I was for thirty years. I'm glad I didn't flip out, because there were several measures I had to take prior to coming out to my co-workers.

I guess by my coming out, I hope to at least educate people about transgender issues. I also fear that someday I will need to call 9-1-1, and I will be treated like the stories that I stated above. By staying quiet, I'm only doing harm to myself and other people like me. I think that I'm in a unique position to help most of the trans-community. In fact, I dedicated a big part of my life to helping people, and this is no different. I can at least show people that we come from normal homes and normal childhoods. We were never molested and nothing specific ever made us this way. We are not just something that just happens on talk shows. I want people to know how inappropriate those comments are considering everything we have to go through. And most of all, we are your friends, your co-workers, your siblings, and your children. I want people to think about how it would feel if somebody called you or your child "it." I want people to know that I was "sick" before my transition, but I'm not sick anymore. I have a completely clear conscience and no skeletons in my closet. I have grown into the person I dreamed of being when I was five. And nobody is ever going to take that away from me. *Ever.*

Now let me tell everyone my future plans at the EMS agency and what I expect from my co-workers. The answer is nothing. If I were to switch roles at work, I would have to deal with every fire department, every police department, every emergency room, every EMS station, every nursing home, and, you get the picture. As I mentioned, this is a very unforgiving group of people, and I don't think I could handle it. I'm not going to request new uniforms, and I'm not going to expect people to call me female pronouns. All I want to do is live out my time at work so I can move onto better things and start a new era of my life. I know that some of you will not accept me, some of you will, and whoever is left will simply not care, but I hope we can coexist at work in peace no matter what your opinions are.

On Thursday night at 2300, I will be back to start my

shift like I normally do, and I'm going to check my truck just like any other shift. I won't be wearing makeup, and I'll probably have my hair tucked up into my hat. I will not mention this to anyone and proceed as I normally do like nothing has changed. I hope people can feel free to say anything they want as long as it's respectful. I'm very open and educated about my situation, and I have no problem answering questions. If you do not accept me and feel that you can't talk to me anymore, that's fine. All I ask is that you respect me as a co-worker and a fellow EMT.

If people want to make comments on here, feel free, and you can e-mail me with any questions, comments, or concerns that you might want to keep private. I will also send pictures upon request via e-mail for those of you who are curious about what I look like when I'm not wearing a badge. Information about transgender issues, success stories, and a lot of information about the subject is also available upon request. And lastly, I do have a sense of humor about who I am. I'm not an uptight bitch that can't take a joke. I just get frustrated when people are mean to those they don't understand.

Sorry this post was so long. I had to tell my story the way I wanted it to be known. Please understand that whatever was said in the past is in the past. I have no hard feelings toward any co-workers or hospital staff. Keep in mind that my co-workers are the only people left in my life that I never told. I have a huge support network of family and friends outside of work, and this is where I got the courage to do what I am doing. Although it's new to you, it's far from new to me. Thank you so very much for taking the time to read this. It really means a lot to me.

Here are some of the responses I received.

May 19, 2009, at 10:11 a.m.
I commend your courage and condemn the narrow-minded. You have my support at work and at the hospital. It is *your* happiness that matters to *you*; don't let anyone at work take that away.

May 19, 2009, at 11:43 a.m.
I am happy for what makes you happy. I was part of that conversation on the pad that night, and I'm sure I said things that might have offended you, so I am very sorry if I hurt your feelings. I had also heard the rumors and thought it was some goofy story, and I'm not sure that I wanted to believe it to be true. I would not say that people here are somewhat ignorant to what you are going through, but completely ignorant ... me included. I don't know the first thing about the transgender process or what kind of inner mental torment you must have gone through, but I do know that you have the biggest set of balls for writing this (include pun). I'm not going to stop busting on you, either. That being said, you are my friend and will always be that no matter what kind of choice you make in your life. I know I can be judgmental, sarcastic, snide, and flat-out rude at times, but I am really proud of you for having the courage to write this down and share it with a group of pretty "unforgiving" people. Public safety providers are a tough crowd!

I hope that you are truly happy, and I can't apologize enough if I offended you. Perhaps some education on what you are going through might open my eyes and give me some perspective. I look forward to talking with you and not because I just want to hear about your new outlook on life and the changes you are going through for my own gain, but because friends are there for friends when they need them. And I guess that when

I heard the rumors, I should have acted like a friend and approached you. It was not something I was comfortable asking you about. I guess I don't need to ask now.

I wrote this to you publicly because I hope it might encourage others to be open minded, as well.

May 20, 2009, at 1:46 a.m.
Jesse,
While I think it is great that you have decided to "come out," as you have put it, I would like to think that it really does not matter to me. By saying that, I am suggesting that I would like to think I consider who you are based on the merit of your actions and not, per se, on your sexuality. I recognize myself in some of your suggestions about intolerant comments, and though I did not intend to offend, it appears that I have, and for that, I am truly sorry. Whether you are Jesse or Jessica, you are part of the midnight family, and I personally would not have it any other way.

May 20, 2009, at 2:21 a.m.
BTW, this was, without question, the "ballsiest" thing I have ever seen anyone do. I can imagine that coming out is difficult for anyone, but for you to lay it all bare like this is an incredible testament to your desire to be appreciated for who you really are. Bravo.

May 21, 2009, at 9:48 a.m.
Jesse:
I agree 100 percent with all the comments that were written before me. It takes great courage to do what you did, and I commend you for that. To me, it doesn't matter if you're Jesse or Jessica; I consider you a friend either way, your preference of who you want to be is your choice, and I will support you in any way. Do

not allow the few who don't understand stop you from being who you really are.

May 22, 2009, at 1:26 a.m.
Jessie,
I just saw this post that you put up. I give you a lot of credit for telling this to the people you work with, especially the group that we work with, including myself. That probably was one of the hardest things that you had to deal with through your life until you finally set the story straight. To be honest with you, I have heard a few stories from people outside of work and thought nothing of them. But there is only one way to find out the true story—by asking someone. But it's hard to ask someone about what you have told us above. I commend you for doing so. Remember we are all a family, no matter how much everyone makes fun of everyone or talks shit behind one another's back. If someone would call anyone from work, I'm 99 percent sure that they would be there to assist in any way that they could. Myself personally, I would not look at you any differently and still consider you a friend.

May 22, 2009, at 9:28 a.m.
Jesse:
I bet this was one of the hardest things that you've ever had to do, and I commend you for doing it. It takes a very strong person with the support of their family and friends to come out and announce this, and I support you 100 percent!

My best friend from high school was gay, but he didn't tell me for almost five years after graduating because he was afraid of how I would react. At first, I was stunned; this was a guy that I partied with, picked girls up with, and all of a sudden, he tells me he is gay and has always had a crush on me. I distanced myself from him for a couple of months but finally realized that he was my friend, and that I should stand by him. We have been out of school for twenty-five years, and we are still good friends, and I would not have it any other way. Stand proud of who you are!

June 9, 2009, at 3:38 p.m.
Jesse,
You have my full and continued support.

# An Interview with Robert Parsons

**How did you become interested in law enforcement?**

My second stepfather, Dan, was a police officer where my mother worked. I have always considered Dan to be one of my biggest role models; he still is to this day even though he's off the job. I grew up in a police household until my parents divorced several years later.

At the age of seven, after sitting in my stepfather's police car for the first time, police work was in my blood. My entire life, I grew up with police officer friends of my mother hanging around the house, and I always knew that it was what I wanted to do. One of my next closest role models growing up, Richard Cash, was a police officer who my mother also worked with. He was killed in the line of duty on January 3, 1996, on a traffic stop in Forest Park, Georgia. Ricky used to let me sit in his patrol car and would let me play with the blue lights as long as I wanted. I will never forget the morning when my mom called home from work to tell me what happened.

I attended his funeral with my mother, and after seeing the thousands of officers present at the service, the honor guards, and all of the vehicles in the procession, I knew that I wanted to be a part of that family.

**When did you discover that you were gay?**

I knew I was gay as far back as my memory takes me, maybe nine or ten, although I did not really understand it until I was around thirteen years old.

When my mother found out, she flipped out. My mother had a relative die of AIDS in the '90s and told me, "I can't see my son go through what he went through." At the time, my mother was an alcoholic and could fly off the handle pretty quickly. She told me once that police officers aren't queer, and that if I chose to be gay, I would never be able to become a police officer.

One time in particular, when I was around fourteen, my mother and I got into an argument. The neighbors called the local police. Two officers showed up. When the police asked my mother what the argument was about, she told them that I was gay, and that if I was gay, I could not live with her.

One of the officers pulled me aside and identified herself to me as a lesbian. This officer, whose name I do not know but often wish I did because I would go find her and give her a hug, explained to me that gays and lesbians are able to become police officers. From that point on, I kept my dream alive and moved forward, just waiting until I turned twenty-one to become old enough to become a police officer.

From the age of eighteen to twenty-one, I worked a few different jobs. I went to EMT school and worked for an ambulance service as a dispatcher and first responder. I also worked as an insurance adjuster for GEICO insurance for a few years. I did very well at GEICO and made more money then than I make now. I knew that if I stayed at GEICO, I could have a very successful career in insurance, and my income potential was outstanding. But all the while, I knew that I wanted to become a police officer, and I might as well do it now before I made too much money to survive the pay cut I was facing if I changed careers.

While at GEICO, I met a man named Russ and fell in love. Russ had an ex-boyfriend named James who was a police officer when Russ and James were together. When I told Russ that I wanted to be a police officer, he became upset and told me that he would not stay with me if I did because when James became a police officer, his entire personality changed and the relationship went to total crap. Well, I said okay and stayed at my insurance job, hating it every day because it wasn't what I wanted to do.

Russ and I found our dream home, and we decided to buy it. The relationship was going okay, and I was actually starting my strategic plan to convince Russ to let me become a police officer. On the day of our house closing and final walk-through, his phone rang. It was a friend named Jason, and he told Russ that James had killed himself in his Atlanta apartment. James was still a police officer at the time of his death and was having problems at work and was just out of a relationship. Life hit James hard, and he decided to end his life. I also knew James before I knew Russ, and I was in total shock. Russ had to leave to go to his mother's while my best friend Gene and I stayed to do the moving of both of our stuff.

What happened in the following months after the funeral eventually led to the demise of my relationship with Russ. After the death of James, It became obvious that my being a police officer and being with Russ were two things that were never going to go together, or so I thought. As the months went on, Russ finally said, "Okay, if it's what you want to do, do it." I made Russ promise that if the job ever became too much for him to take, he would let me know and let me decide on what to do before he made the "I'm leaving" decision. Russ agreed, and off I ran to the computer to find out who was hiring in the area.

I had a friend who worked for a college police department in Atlanta who told me that they were hiring four people. I wasn't sure that the "college cop" thing was what I wanted to do, but then I thought, *It might be a college, but it's still in downtown Atlanta, so I'm sure it will be okay, and I'll get my fun and excitement.* As I would find out later, boy, was I right!

I applied, and the hiring process moved on pretty quickly. Application, interview, lie-detector test, background check, credit check, driver's history, psych test, POST test, physical ... the normal stuff. Within two months, I got the job, and I couldn't turn in my notice at the insurance company fast enough. Sadly enough, I was so excited that I didn't exactly finish my two weeks at the insurance company because, after all, I had to get ready and had too many gadgets and belt accessories to find before the academy. Yup ... I was one of them!

My academy dates got pushed back two months, so I just hung

around the police station waiting to go to the police academy. I washed cars, let the department's K-9 units use me as a bite bad boy, cleaned out the outside garage, and moved furniture.

Finally, I'm off to the academy. Day One, "Black Monday," was a wake-up call. Instructors in my face, push-ups, running ... oh, what did I get myself in to? The academy moved by pretty quickly, and I walked away with the "Top Driver" award. I was stoked. There was a guy in my class who I went to high school with who knew that I was gay. I had not seen him in years. I never told anyone in the academy that I was gay, at least not while I was there. I doubt he told anyone, either. So, during the academy, as far as I know, no one knew about me.

I started with a training officer who was a very country, Southern Baptist—not that there is anyone wrong with Baptists, it's just that, historically, they are not LGBT people's biggest fans—so needless to say, I wasn't coming out. We spent hours a day looking at women and such. Hearing "queer," etc., come out of his mouth happened often and I never really minded too much I guess, although I felt as if I were selling my soul to the devil for not speaking out. I eventually became great friends with my FTO, and I respect him as a police officer.

As time went on and I got out on my own, people started to find out. There were other openly gay officers at the department who had seen me out, and I guess they started to tell, but by this point, I believe that I had already earned the respect of most of my co-workers. I have been treated no differently than anyone else at the department. I am friends with almost everyone there, and we have several openly gay and lesbian officers at the department, including a lesbian captain, Regina, who has been a wonderful role model to me, and a gay detective, Justin, who is a little over the top but a great friend all the same.

I am by far the most proactive officer on my patrol squad, and I have several great friends on my team. My shift supervisor, Lewis, has also become a great role model to me and a close friend, and even though he is from a little country town in Louisiana, he is very accepting of me being gay.

I met my soul mate on my shift, Candy. Well, maybe not *soul mate*, but she sure feels like it sometimes. Candy looks after me like no one else, and God help someone who ever tried to mess with me. And trust me when I say that I feel the same way about her.

My mother died on April 25, 2008, and the support I received from my department was phenomenal. I was at the state police academy taking a class when I phone rang with the news. It was 500 percent unexpected. I left the academy that morning upset, in shock, and heading for my sister's, and I picked up the phone and called Candy. Candy was at my sister's at almost the same time I was and did not leave for several days. The department motors unit escorted the funeral, and there were about twenty-five officers present from my department, including my chief, Teresa, who is a wonderful person and who I would follow anywhere.

Losing my mother was probably one of the hardest things I have ever had to go through, and having such a supportive department really has made it easier for me. My mother and I had developed a wonderful relationship, and she was my best friend and by far my number-one fan. She loved my ex-boyfriends and became very accepting of my sexuality and my career choice, even though she worried about me daily and would call every night I worked to check up on me. I learned quickly that I always better answer the phone, or Mom's calling dispatch!

I still worry about being discriminated against by other officers and the public at large. It has not happened to me that often, but it has happened. I also know that if I ever choose to leave the big-city department, it would not be such a positive experience. I have friends all over the state of Georgia who are in the closet and are miserable with their departments.

I guess I am the lucky one, even though I probably will not ever be able to work out in the country areas where I am from and where I am the happiest in general. Big-city life isn't for me, but I make the most of it.

**What would you have done differently?**
I would have come out in the academy to some of the close friends I made.

**What advice do you have for young LGBT teens?**
Don't give up! No matter what anyone tells you, you can do it and be

very successful at it. Go to work for a department in an area where there are gay police officer alliances and places where you are less likely to have a negative experience. Find a role model or mentor that can help you with the process. Go to college, if you can, and get a degree first. If not, come on, anyway.

**What advice do you have about coming out at work?**
Come out, or not, when you're ready. If you are unhappy with your department, find a new place to work where you feel that you can be who you are. Life is too short to try to be something you're not. I know it must be hard to leave somewhere you are use to working, but your happiness is key, and there are so many departments out there where you can be yourself and never have to worry about being discriminated against.

**What advice do you have for chiefs and sheriffs?**
Form LGBT officer organizations for your officers. If not that, at least allow your officers to be who they are and do not tolerate discrimination in the workplace based on someone's sexual orientation. Gays and lesbians make great police officers, and they are worth keeping around. I have never met a lazy or ineffective LGBT police officer. Make sure your supervisors, administrators, civilian employees, and officers understand that discrimination will not be tolerated.

# An Interview with Bill

I am twenty years old and a volunteer firefighter and EMT in West Virginia. I am part of the attack crew with the fire department, and I am one of the five emergency medical technicians at our station. There is a big need for volunteers, and it makes it hard to go out on calls and handle it ourselves, so we use mutual aid a lot in the area.

I am scared to come out to the other members at my station because I fear what would happen. They have run people out of our town just because they were black, and I can only imagine what they would do if they found out that I am bisexual. It just makes it hard to try to go out on calls to try to help my community in their time of need when I cannot be myself.

**How did you become interested in emergency medical services?**
Most of the men in my family have been firefighters at one time or another, so I heard a lot about the fire department growing up. I didn't decide to join until my dad died about three years ago. The day he died is the day I decided to join the fire department and try to help save someone's life. Even if I could only keep a patient alive for a couple of

minutes, I could at least give the family members their last good-byes to their loved one.

**When did you discover that you were bisexual?**
I knew that I was bisexual when I was in middle school. I never really pursued it out of fear of being different. I always would look at guys but never tried anything with another man until I was in high school. That is when more people around me started to come out and be open about their sexuality. Sadly, there are not many gay, lesbian, or bisexual people in the fire and emergency medical services in the area in which I live and work, so it is still new to a lot of people.

**What was your basic training experience like?**
I am a volunteer, so we take classes around our work schedule. I have taken multiple firefighting classes, including hazmat, NEMS, and safety officer. I am also in the process of becoming a CPR instructor and hope to start helping teach EMT-B classes soon after that.

**How did you come out at work?**
When I first joined, I felt like an outcast. It took a while to get over that feeling. For the first couple months, my co-workers were trying to figure out if I was gay or straight. Finally, after about four months, I really started to feel like a real member there. Most of the people that avoided me at first were the older members of the department. I know they don't agree with two men or women being together. We can do anything that they can do; they just need to give us the chance, and we can prove our abilities to them.

I've told a couple of my close friends about me, but I am afraid of how the rest of my co-workers will accept it. I love being there for the community and being there to try to help people, and I don't want to give that up. I have put most of my time into this to try to get trained, so I don't want to lose it all just because some people don't agree with how people live.

**What has been the most difficult situation you've faced at work?**
The most difficult time I have ever had was on an EMS call about three

months ago. It was a call for a domestic violence situation with a married couple that was drunk. The man must have pushed the woman, and she broke her ankle. I was the only EMT there, and I only had two other people at first to help me other than the law enforcement officers on the scene. Both of the officers were trying to arrest the male half of the incident.

When we walked in, I introduced myself to the woman as an EMT and started to ask her some questions. She started to call me all sorts of names and stated that she didn't want a "fag" to touch her. Apparently, she was the mother of one of the guys that I used to be close to, so she knew about me, and because of her, we had to break it off. It was hard to take all that and still try to help this woman out when she saying so many things that I didn't want the other members to know while also calling me all sorts of names.

After we took her to the hospital, several of my co-workers started to question me on what this woman was saying. I tried to cover it up, but I really think that most of the members know about me now, and the two guys that were there have never really treated me the same since then. They don't run calls with us anymore, so things are getting back to normal now, but it's hard to try to live two lives and lie to so many people just to try to fit in.

**What advice do you have for young people wanting to get into the EMS profession?**
If you want to get into public safety, don't be afraid to go for it. I'm not going to sit here and say that it might not be hard at times, because it might be, but don't let people stop you from doing something that you love to do. There are always going to be people around you that will help support you the entire time.

**What advice do you have about coming out at work?**
I know very well how hard it is to be bisexual and not be out to people at the station. Just keep doing your best, and whenever you feel safe enough to tell people, do it. Don't be afraid to take your time and go at your own speed.

# AN INTERVIEW WITH KYLE ROSS

I am a thirty-five-year-old male in the central United States and currently work in law enforcement. I have experience in firefighting and EMS, as well.

**How did you become interested in law enforcement?**
I became interested in firefighting at a very young age. For as long as I can remember, I would chase the fire trucks down the street and dream of being the fire chief. I began with a volunteer fire department locally when I was younger and moved into a paid fire department. I then got a taste of law enforcement through some friends and have been in law enforcement ever since and love it!

**When did you discover that you were gay?**
I have always known that I was gay. As a young, young child, I remember looking at guys and thinking, "Wow!" when all my friends were ogling over girls. Being from a small town, I didn't dare to tell anyone that I was gay. My small community was notorious as a KKK town in the past (as early as the '50s), and it is a rural, farming community that did

not seem like the place for a gay, let alone a gay cop! I had accepted the fact that to stay with my current department, I would never be happy in my personal life, but I was on the fast track to promotions. I cheated myself out of years of my own happiness using my job, goals, and accomplishments as an excuse.

### Were you "out" in the academy?

I was not out in the academy. I actually graduated the academy and became very well known in my area. I was liked by all of the officers, always willing to help other officers, and I quickly moved up in my department. I was promoted to shift commander only two and a half years out of the academy at age twenty-three. I did not want to mess up what I had going.

### How did you come out at work?

The longer I worked in my agency, the more and more I longed for a personal relationship to make me happy. I dated girls, my friends hooked me up, and I did all the things that you would think a young, single, good-looking cop should be doing. My agency is small (less than thirty sworn), and I hear the gay jokes, innuendos, etc. I never considered coming out here! I applied at agencies in surrounding states that I thought were more liberal but could never leave here.

Finally, in 2003, it was time to come out at age twenty-eight. I had tested the waters online by looking at gay profiles, using chat rooms, etc. I always started talking to guys but then would get scared that they were learning too much about me and thought they could identify me, so I would stop talking to them. One night, I talked on a chat to a guy who said he was from a large metro area about twenty miles from me. As we chatted, I said something (I don't remember now what it was), and he immediately made the link and started asking questions about my city and agency. Boy, did that freak me out! I stopped talking to him. I was at work one night and was approached by this guy, and I swore it was not me.

As time went on, I guess I got lonelier and lonelier. I tried contacting another guy locally. This time, I got the guts to call and talk to the guy on the phone, but I drove around while talking to him and made sure I was out of my city so that "they" couldn't hear me. I don't know who "they" would be, but it made me feel better. I ended up meeting this guy and had my first real relationship. I remained closeted at work, but now people were asking questions. I was always around, both on and off duty, and now no one knew where I was for a week or two at a time off duty. One officer I work with is very nosy, and the rumors started spreading.

I was terrified of losing my friends, family, co-workers, and the respect of the community I grew up in—and I had been a rather high-profiled officer for years. I remember vividly my mother asking me if I had a girlfriend during this time, and I said no. She then asked if I had a boyfriend, and I replied, "Don't ask questions you don't want to know the answer to!"

Things just kind of fell into place. I told my family (they knew—they always knew!). I then started telling my closest friends. One of my closest friends was very redneck, and I knew he would have issues with this—so I waited to tell him! After about a month, everyone I was close to knew. We started going places together. My chief learned about it, as did the rest of my co-workers. You know what? To my surprise, all of them told me that it was not a big deal. Being gay is not *who* I am; it is a *part* of me. I don't flaunt it, but I also don't lie about it if I am asked directly. The rumor also got out around town. Several people I know asked me about it and were cool with it when I told them. I can honestly say that I have not lost any friends, family, or co-workers over coming out. I do know a couple of people that are still on edge about it, but they are cool to my face.

Long story short, that relationship was bad! The guy used me for money and a place to live. I broke it off with him and basically went into hiding for a month or so. Then I met the greatest guy I have ever met. We met online (yeah, I know the stigma, but it was my only option in my mind) in late 2003, and we have been together for seven years now. We bought a house together in a beautiful neighborhood. Our neighbors love us. We go everywhere together, including work functions, and everyone is very supportive of our relationship. Good times and more ahead to come!

### What is the most difficult situation you have faced on the job?
My most difficult situation while on duty has been when I arrest drunks

and disorderly people who know I am gay. They make comments, call me a "faggot," and put me down. It is funny, though, that when they are sober, they talk to me with respect and don't even blink at my sexuality.

One story does come to mind, and at the time, it made me incredibly sad. We ran a "Code Blue," which is a patient who is not breathing and has no pulse. It was a female in her twenties that had overdosed on some pills. A female had called in the incident and was screaming on the phone to the point where dispatch thought this was a disturbance. I arrived, and we performed CPR on the victim, who ultimately died. I learned that the other female was her partner. Over the next month, I received calls almost daily from the deceased female's mother. There was a huge pissing match between her and the partner. Basically, it boiled down to the fact that the mother didn't accept the daughter's lifestyle, and now she felt guilty. They were arguing over property, money, everything. I finally told the mother that I could not help her with these issues and that the death was ruled accidental/suicide, and the calls stopped. A few months later, while doing bar checks, I saw the partner at the bar. I did not recognize her, but she asked if she could speak to me. We went outside, and she began crying. She told me that she needed to thank me, that she knows that I have a job to do, and that I would not show emotion, but I had treated her with respect, and it meant the world to her that day. She hugged me and said that every time she sees me, she sees an angel. I about lost it! I told my partner about this later, and still it brings me to tears.

Why does society have to be so unaccepting? It's not right, and then once someone loses someone with whom they drove a wedge over something like this, they really regret it. Thank God for my friends and family. Thank God!

**What has been your most surprising experience?**
Without question, it has been the acceptance of the community. Everyone I have talked to said that they were shocked to learn that I was gay, but they are happy for me. They ask my partner's name, how he is doing, and they treat me like we are any normal, happy family. Oh, wait … we are!

**Would you have done anything differently?**

Other than wishing I could have come out years ago, I would not have done anything differently. The best thing I did was to be honest about who I am—first with myself and second with those I care for—both at home and at work. I remember shortly after I came out at work, I was approached by an older but lower-ranking officer. Somehow, we got on the topic of trust and officers being honest. I remember that officer telling me that I was "golden" with him after the way I handled coming out. He told me that I did not go off the deep end exclaiming my sexuality, but when someone asked, I also respected them enough not to lie to them. I remember him telling me that he did not think he could be that strong about little things, let alone something like this! That really solidified that I had done the right thing. I am now thought of as someone that can be told anything and it will never be repeated. I have also been told by several people that they could see me being a chief in the future.

Coming out earlier would have made my life so much happier! I never saw it, but after I came out and met my partner, a dear friend of mine told my partner that I was a "dick" and everybody "hated me" before I came out. They said I was tough, had no sympathy, and that I was arrogant. She (and others) said that they noticed a day-and-night difference almost overnight when I met my partner. It truly was a great thing for me.

**What advice can you offer LGBT youth interested in law enforcement?**

First, get educated! You can never have too much education. Go as far as you can—you will need it. Second, be yourself and stand on your integrity, honesty, values, and morals. Being gay is *what* you are; it is not *who* you are! The world doesn't owe you anything! You are gay, I know. Work hard, play hard, and be happy. You will go far in working hard, sticking to your integrity, and letting people know that you are a man or woman of your word. People get a bad taste when anyone (gay or straight) thinks that the world owes them something. I learned this early on, and I am very blessed to be where I am in life. Could I make more money? Yes. Could I have better benefits? Yes. But, ultimately, it was my decision to be a cop and to work where I work, and I love it. Money isn't everything.

Finally, find an ally. *You will need one!* Whether family, friend, or someone you read about and contact through this book, talk to someone. As Chief David O'Malley said, "Being a cop is tough! Being a gay cop is tougher." You can't do it alone; no one can! The world will be just as accepting of you as you want them to be and let them be.

## What advice do you have about coming out at work?

Unfortunately, only you know when the time is right to come out. I would encourage you to do it, though. I did it and in a town of under ten thousand people—a rural farming community full of rednecks. You know what? It worked for me! You will have to do it at your pace, but keep in mind that time is wasting, and you are missing a lot of great times that you will never get back. I would not try to talk anyone into coming out if they were not 110 percent ready. Bad things could happen; you should know that. I am sure—no, I am *positive*—that I am very, very, very lucky with my situation. But, I am also positive that *you* can find your place in the world. Maybe it is not where you are now, but there is a place for you. Find an ally, communicate with someone. You will not believe the rush of excitement and weight off your shoulders when you are not worried about whether someone sees you out at a movie with some guy or gal.

## What advice can you offer chiefs and sheriffs?

*Good for you!* Don't be afraid to ask questions or to talk to your employee(s). I know it is awkward and you don't know what to say, but talk to them. My chief always asks how my partner is doing. I know he tries even though I also know that he doesn't know what to ask or say. I can't tell you how much I love to talk about what my partner is doing and how well we are doing as a couple.

Also, whatever you do, don't change because of us. I have heard all the gay jokes, comments, etc. After I came out, they continued. Some say this is sexual harassment. I say bullshit! These are guys being guys. I don't want to walk in a room and have everyone go silent or think about what they are saying so they don't offend me. You won't offend me; if you do, I will tell you. No harm, no foul. This goes back to my philosophy that the world doesn't owe me anything! I owe it to the world to do what I can while I am here. I also owe it to my friends to let them be them, just as they let me be me. Go ahead, make jokes; I will probably even join in. Don't make us feel like outsiders; that makes it even harder, and we need to be a part of our law enforcement family.

If you are not out, I commend you. You are living one of the absolutely toughest lives that there is in existence. Keep working toward it; it will get easier. If you are out, *congratulations!* It is likely the hardest thing you have ever done, gone through, or will ever go through. What doesn't kill you makes you stronger (they tell me). If you are an ally who is straight, *good for you!* I really don't care who you are, what you are about, what religion you are, or where you are from. We should all be treated equally.

# REPLACING SHAME WITH PRIDE

I was standing in the office of San Francisco Mayor Gavin Newsome with my husband Tony. We were both there by invitation to watch the annual raising of the gay pride flag over city hall. I'm guessing that there was about one hundred other people there mixed among members of the board of supervisors and the other elected City of San Francisco officials. A band was playing in the rotunda, and the San Francisco Gay Men's Choir is preparing for their performance. There was energy in the air, a sense of celebration, excitement, and pride.

The mayor emerged from his office. He looked just like I had seen him on television many times. Although not nearly as tall as I thought, the hair, the suit, the smile, and his enthusiasm were all perfectly aligned for the event. He led the crowd to his balcony on the second floor of city hall. He called back, summoning members of the board of supervisors to join him at the flagpole, which protruded up at an angle off the balcony. Then, as if he and the other civic leaders were cutting the ribbon at the opening of a new building, they tossed up the brightly colored rainbow flag, and the crowd broke into applause. Mayor Newsome exclaimed, "Happy Pride, everyone!"

We all left the mayor's office and assembled on the steps of the second floor looking out into the rotunda. The choir sang the "Star-Spangled Banner" and "San Francisco." And as I listened to the music and then the dozen or so speeches from the mayor and the other elected officials who are gay and out, I stood in wonder thinking about how, just forty years ago, none of this would have been possible.

Being gay in 1969 usually meant hiding in shame. There was nothing to celebrate, no pride flag to raise, and certainly no elected officials who were gay. Well, none who were "out," anyway. In 1969, I was in the first grade. I remember having a huge crush on a boy in my class named Chip. His mother was my teacher and didn't like me much. In fact, she tried to hold me back a grade. Maybe I spent too much time thinking about Chip. Of course, I didn't know what being gay was then and didn't know anything about a bar in New York called the "Stonewall Inn." I had no idea that a group of drag queens would rise up against the police and society as a whole and create what we now know as "gay pride." As I stood there in city hall thinking about those pioneers who decided to feel shame no more, I started really thinking about why gay pride celebrations are so important.

I knew that I was gay by the time I first walked into the boys' locker room in seventh grade. While I may not have known the word for it, I knew that who I was attracted to was very different from my male classmates (well, at least most them). It was the same time that I learned being "queer" or a "fag" was the worst of all things. The school I attended was located in an upper-middle-class community that was almost all white. You could be overweight, of a different race, unusually tall or short, a "geek," or a "snitch" and still be in better standing with your peers than if you were gay.

Everyone in seventh grade was called a "fag" at one time or another, but those like me who were not athletic or part of the "in" crowd heard it all the time. Being called that name and knowing that, in fact, I *was* gay created a deep-rooted feeling of shame that has taken me years to shed.

I never realized until well after I came out how damaging and demoralizing feeling shame can be. Gay pride is the polar opposite of this shame and its origin. Until you have felt this shame, I would imagine it would be quite difficult to really feel why pride celebrations are so important. The fact that these celebrations today include participation from straight leaders and prominent politicians is remarkable. In fact, in 1999, President Clinton became the first president in history to issue a presidential proclamation designating the month of June as National Gay Pride Month. President Obama continued this tradition in 2009. In that proclamation, President Obama recognized the bravery of those who really started the gay rights movement at Stonewall as well as the many contributions of gay and lesbian people over the last forty years. For me, this kind of recognition and celebration is an important part of defeating decades of deeply engrained shame.

Fortunately, times are changing rapidly. Like almost every other area of our society, attitudes about homosexuality are evolving in such away that someday being gay will not cause someone to feel shame to the extent that it has and does for many today. If you look back to just forty years ago, you will see that being out meant being almost a complete outcast, being prohibited from being employed by any government agency, and not being able to marry anywhere. Today, with the exception of the military, you can serve in a government position at the local, state, or federal level and be completely out as a gay or lesbian person. You can get married to your same-sex partner in five states.

Today it is so very possible to be out and to live an authentic life. Anyone with a sexual orientation different from the "norm" has the opportunity to live a full and complete life in the truth free from having to hide and lie about a very important part of life. Today it is truly possible to move from a feeling of shame to one of pride. This section of the book is really all about that journey and how it can be in the twenty-first century.

I've written this part of the book based on my own experience and research, including input from the many gay and straight friends I've met along the way. I wrote about my own coming-out experience in my first book, *Coming Out from Behind the Badge*. I came out later in life largely out of fear of being rejected by my profession and my family. I started my law enforcement career very early at the age of fifteen as a police explorer. I learned within hours of walking into the police department that being gay in law enforcement was not possible. The slurs and comments I heard from my young peers as well as from the officers I met fueled the bigotry and hate of homosexuality I had learned in school, from the media, and from society as a whole. I spent twenty-six years trying to hide who I really am while working for three different law enforcement agencies in positions from 9-1-1 dispatcher all the way up to deputy chief.

I also became a part-time teacher at three different police academies located on community college campuses in California. Although these institutions of higher education were already light-years ahead of law enforcement in their acceptance of homosexuality, the police culture was alive and well within the law enforcement programs. And because all of these teaching positions were literally "at will," I never felt that I could take the risk of being myself even at these colleges. Teaching for me is my life's true vocation. I knew that I wanted to be a teacher long before I discovered law enforcement. I love the classroom and my students, and the thought of being excluded from that opportunity was not something I cared to risk for the sake of being able to come out and live an authentic life.

In 1999, I was hired by Napa Valley College as the full-time director of the police academy there. I had been working with this college since 1986, almost from the time the academy was created there. The selection process was highly political and sensitive because just a year before the position opened, the program was nearly shutdown by the state. The selection process involved many local and state high-ranking law enforcement personnel, faculty from the college, and the college president herself. To this day, I don't believe that I would have been selected if I was out, but then again, a lot has changed in the last ten years.

I knew that there were rumors about me almost from the very beginning of my career. As I got older and more successful, the rumors grew. No one ever confronted me directly, but I knew that there was a lot of talking going on behind my back. Despite all of the pain these rumors caused every time I heard one, I never felt pressure to come out and always feared the worst if I did. My career meant more to me than my own personal happiness, but as time went on, I felt a growing emptiness and loneliness that I knew I couldn't continue. It wasn't that I never met men or dated at all—it was that I kept my personal and sexual life completely separate from all other parts of my life. I was, by all counts, living two lives, and I did everything I could to keep them completely separate. The numerous one-night stands were exciting and fun but usually empty and void of any real feelings of intimacy. As I think back on it now, I took some incredible risks meeting people at their homes or in places where anything could have happened. I never let anyone I met know my real name, what I did for a living, or where I lived. I didn't exchange phone numbers, and I used aliases to protect myself from anyone knowing that I worked in law enforcement. While there was a lot of short-lived excitement in all of this, I knew that I wanted more out of life, and I began to search for a way to come out.

In 2001, I became involved with the Matthew Shepard Foundation and developed a great friendship with Matthew's mother, Judy Shepard. If you aren't familiar with the story, Matthew was a college student at the University of Wyoming who happened to be gay. He was abducted and murdered because he was gay in October of 1998 (for more information, go to www.matthewshepard.org). Judy speaks all over the country about hate crimes and about her son. I remember her saying over and over again how it important it is for every gay and lesbian person to come out and to tell their stories. I owe a lot of being able to find my way out of the closet to Matthew and Judy.

I prayed for several years for someone to come into my life that I could come out to, and in March of 2004, someone did. Like almost everyone who comes out after hiding for such a long time, I felt a sense of relief and freedom that is hard to put into words. It was a feeling like no other that I had experienced in my forty-one years of life to date. I felt whole but also very scared of what was ahead of me. I realized that I now had to undo more than twenty-five years of lies and deceit and had to face a demon called shame.

Admitting to myself that I was gay and saying it out loud for the first time was challenging enough, but now facing the need to tell friends and my parents seemed overwhelming. I waited for several months to tell anyone as I worked with myself to begin tearing down the wall of separation I had built to divide and protect my two lives. Fortunately, I had sage advice from the person I came out to and started to build a group of gay friends. I found the conversations we had to be invaluable and so reaffirming. What I was feeling was not unique, and hearing the stories of others—how they told friends, their parents, and co-workers—really helped me configure a strategy for how I was going to approach those in my own life.

I also began to read every book I could find on gay life and coming out. I read hundreds of coming-out stories from teachers, college students, and athletes. Like hearing the coming-out stories of my friends, these stories were very helpful in giving me perspective and a sense of how to be successful. I no longer felt isolated or alone. But the feelings of shame were still deeply rooted inside me. I remember speaking for the Matthew Shepard Foundation at UC Davis. I was sitting on a panel with several other gay people and the county sheriff, who was straight. During the presentation, I never identified myself as being gay and talked mostly about hate crimes and how police are trained to respond. The sheriff knew of me from my role as the director of the academy. After the program, he asked, "So, are you a member of the gay community?" Even though I had come out months earlier, I immediately responded, "No." The sense of shame, fear, and internalized homophobia I felt was very much in control. I know I didn't answer out of habit; it was a conscious response based on the need I felt to protect myself. This situation bothered me for several days, but it helped me discover one important part of the coming-out process that I really needed to deal with, and it was clear to me that it was going to be a true personal challenge.

It was three months after formally coming out for the first time that I told another friend in my life. I can remember to this day how nervous and how fearful I was of losing my friend. I completely underestimated his reaction. It went so well that I told a second friend that same afternoon. My experience with these first two friends gave me the confidence to continue telling my friends and eventually my parents. Talking to my sister and mother was fairly easy. I dreaded telling my father because I assumed that he would not react well. While I think my assumptions were logically based on the fact he is a devoted Catholic and thirty-year career firefighter, I was blown away by his acceptance and embrace. For all of this, I am truly thankful.

From the minute I came out, I started to approach dating and relationships completely differently than at any time before. I was honest about who I was and started looking for people to meet based on other characteristics than those desirable for a one-night stand. In December of that same year, I met Tony. We grew together quickly and fell in love over the course of that following year. I proposed to him a year later in Hawaii, and we were married in Canada in July of 2006. We bought a house together the following year and continue to grow as a couple. While I attribute the start of my journey of coming out to Judy Shepard, I must give Tony the credit for guiding me away from shame to a place of personal pride.

I offer this very brief story about me so that you can understand my perspective on what I write about in this section of the book. This part of the book is intended to be a guide for coming out in the twenty-first century. So much has changed in society since you discovered that you were gay. Even if you made this discovery just a year ago, the world is becoming a better and more accepting place for gay and lesbian people. But we still have a long way to go, and society as it is still causes us to feel shame about who we are. As a minority—and we will always be that—we are struggling for the same basic rights the majority enjoys. There are still negative stereotypes and stigmas about gay people that feed the shame we feel. Gay people are still the third-most-common victim of hate crimes, and most states still do not have laws prohibiting employment discrimination based on sexual orientation.

This section of the book is about what I've experienced and researched since coming out in 2004. It is written for anyone who is at any point in the process of coming out. I hope the friends and family members of those who are gay, lesbian, bisexual, or transgender will also read it. However, I should explain now that sexual orientation and gender identity are two entirely different issues that may or may not be connected. I have never questioned my gender identity and cannot attest to that experience. I have included what I have learned about gender identity, but this book is not about coming out as transgender or any part of the transition process. I don't feel qualified to even speculate about that experience. These are my ideas about how to grow from a place of feeling shame to one of feeling proud to be who you are. It is my hope that I can share with you how you can live an authentic and true life as a gay, lesbian, or bisexual person here in the twenty-first century.

I've written this section to stand alone while, of course, directly relating to the overall theme of this book. I've included websites and resources that you can explore further based on your own interests and needs. All of these resources are ones that I have used at one point or another in my life. Of course, every individual is different, and your life experience may be vastly different from mine. I realize that not everything I suggest or recommend will be right for every reader, but they are my own perspectives and experiences, and I ask only that you consider them, as they may benefit and help you in your own situation.

It is important to talk about terminology and how I will use certain words throughout this section of the book. There is a collection of slang terminology associated with homosexuality and its culture that is worthy enough of its own dictionary. How appropriate or inappropriate these words are is largely generational. For example, the words, *gay*, *queer*, and *fairy* have all been used at different points in time as the common word to describe a homosexual. *Queer* has also been inclusive of bisexual and transgender people. I remember in high school hearing the word *queer-bait* used. What the hell is a *queer-bait*? I guess that means you are bait for queers? Thirty years ago, *queer* was a very derogatory word, but today it is the word of choice for many young people to describe their own sexuality.

For the purposes of this section of the book, I'm going to use *gay* to refer to nonheterosexuals. This may cause grief for some of you, but in my generation, the word *queer* was used in the same context and with the same violence as *fag*. It's just not a word I'm comfortable with. I realize that the younger generations are less comfortable with the term *gay* and that *queer* is a term more broadly understood to include homosexuals, bisexuals, pansexuals, intersexed, and those questioning their sexuality. Humor me and understand that within this context of this section, *gay* is inclusive of all nonheterosexual orientations except in those cases where I specify otherwise. I will use the word *straight* to refer to heterosexuals. I'm not sure why *straight* has been coined by society to refer to heterosexuals and why we don't use *crooked* or *bent* or *round* for nonheterosexuals. But *straight* is the recognized term, and it will work just fine for this discussion.

I like the word *authentic* because it means real, honest, true, pure, and original. For something, or someone, to be authentic, there are no lies, no deceit, no cover-ups, no fictitious names, no need to for hidden parts of yourself. Certainly, we all play different roles in our lives depending on the context. For example, at work, a person who is a manager has a role as a leader, disciplinarian, and visionary, but at home, that same person may be a wife, husband, partner, second-income earner, or any number of roles opposite or different from the one at work. So many pieces of our personality transcend all of the roles we have in life, and one of those is our sexual orientation.

Replacing shame with pride is the process of coming out and integrating sexual orientation with all of the various roles you have in life. Coming out is not something you decide to do one time and then wipe the sweat off your brow and say, "Okay, I'm done." Coming out is a lifelong process because you will do it over and over again. You can be the most "out" gay activist in the world, and you will go through a coming-out process with every conversation about your personal life you have with someone you've never met before. Because being gay means being different from the majority of people in the world, gay people become the exception to the rule. This is true of any minority group. But one thing that is different from, say, a minority race, is that you can't see sexual orientation.

The coming-out process begins way before a watercooler conversation at work. It really begins inside the individual wherein the person comes out to himself or herself and begins to identify his or her own sexual orientation. Society has developed definitions and labels for the variety of sexual orientations that exist, and connecting with one of those labels helps you identify who you are. Because society has such a negative history with nonheterosexual orientations, discovering this identity can be riddled with fear, denial, and self-rejection. The most common emotion is a feeling of shame, and overcoming this negative feeling is essential to coming out and staying out.

Once you come out to yourself, the next step is to figure out how to share this aspect of your being with everyone in your life. Part of this decision is figuring out who to tell and how to tell them. There are so many different ways of doing it depending on the relationships and history involved. Certainly, younger people who have never denied who they are or who have never lied about being gay don't have the same cross to bear with family and friends. People who are coming out later in life most often have two layers of coming out to deal with. The first layer is telling people that they are gay, and the second is explaining all the lies for so many years.

What I've found is that every individual person in your life has a unique relationship and history with you. Therefore, there is no one rock-solid method of coming out that you can use for everyone in your life. In this chapter, I will talk about all of these issues and offer some suggestions based on my own experience about how to manage these important relationships through the coming-out process. Most importantly in this section are the thoughts and ideas about how to rid yourself of feeling shameful about being gay. It's a tall order and an effort that can take years of work to fill. Shame manifests itself in mysterious and unseen ways at times. Even the most confident of persons can regress and experience shame. I think this is one area where listening to the experiences and stories of others really helps.

Before reading any further, let me say that I don't mean to sound "preachy" in this book. It's tough to write what is largely a self-help section and not do some preaching, but my intent is only to share my experience and ideas. I do consider myself to be a "professional" gay person, but certainly I cannot speak for every gay person or for the gay culture as a whole. My formal education is not in psychology, but as a teacher and law enforcement officer for most all of my adult life, I have experience that gives me a perspective that cannot be learned in a formal educational setting.

My experience is my own, and I offer it to you as you read for your benefit and consideration. If what I say causes you to disagree, great, because it is also causing you to think. I certainly hope that I don't offend anyone, but if I do, learn from my negative example. Share what you read and what you learn from me with those in your life. Talk about your differences, how you see the world, what it feels like, and how you react to it. The value is not in finding agreement with others, but in the discussion itself.

## How to Come Out

I got a call this morning from a young guy from the Midwest named Mike who was absolutely terrified after finding out that a student in one of his college classes had found his profile on a gay professionals website. Mike told me that he was out to only a few of his friends and feared that word about him would spread. Mike was not out to his mother yet, and he wanted her to know from him rather than hearing about it from someone else. He was also very concerned about his co-workers and boss finding out about him. Mike loves his job and is planning a career in the same field.

What really struck me about Mike's story is that here it is 2010, and a guy in his early twenties was experiencing the exact same fears I did back in 1978. If you think we've come further than that, think again. Coming out as something other than a heterosexual is still very challenging and can be scary no matter your age. But coming out starts with you first, inside your own being, and so that is where I will start.

I remember as far back as third grade having feelings for another boy in my class named Ricky. They weren't sexual feelings, but more of wanting to be his friend or to have him as a brother. I couldn't put a name to those feelings, and they never bothered me or made me question why I was different. In fact, I wasn't aware of any other boys who had a crush on a girl, because at that age, boys wanted to be with boys, and girls wanted to be friends with girls. It all just seemed right.

In sixth grade, I remember Vince and Dana being the first official "boy-girl" couple of our class, and I think it was then that I started to realize that I was more interested in Vince than Dana. I remember seeing them kiss on the playground. It felt like there was a crowd around them, and this kiss was the subject of great gossip among the sixth graders at my school. I was never interested in kissing Dana, but I remember being very interested in what kissing Vince would be like.

Everyone, gay or straight, can probably recall the first feeling of attraction to another person very early in life. Maybe it was first grade, third grade, or even in junior high. You probably couldn't have explained it or rationalized it—it just *was*. Your attraction was not a conscious choice to make, but it was likely a feeling or emotion that you felt. When you look at a group of people and say who is good looking, you are reacting to a visual response from your brain. This is anything but a cognitive or learned process. It is as much of an innate characteristic as is your hair color, skin tone, or shoe size. The sex you are attracted to comes from the same place, but it may not be as black-and-white as society has defined it to be. In other words, there is great variety and degrees of attraction ranging from exclusively a same-sex attraction to exclusively an opposite sex attraction. Your sexual orientation is what gender you are attracted to sexually.

We have a real need in our society to put labels on people and things. We created boxes that often create an "either/or" situation that doesn't work well for identifying and labeling aspects of personality like sexual orientation. In fact, many psychologists who have studied human sexuality have confirmed that there is a wide spectrum of sexual orientation. Perhaps the most famous psychologist to study sexuality was Alfred Kinsey. He published two famous studies, *Sexual Behavior in the Human Male* in 1948 and *Sexual Behavior in the Human Female* in 1953. In 2005, a movie, *Kinsey*, was made about the life of this famous psychologist and about his studies.

What Kinsey found was that 37 percent of males and 13 percent of females said they had at least some distinct homosexual experience that resulted in an orgasm. According to his studies, 10 percent of males and 2–6 percent of females identified as being more or less exclusively homosexual. Based on his study, Kinsey devised the now famous "Kinsey Scale," which proposes that sexual orientation is a continuum ranging from one to six—one being exclusively heterosexual and six being exclusively homosexual. It was from Kinsey's original work and the studies of others who followed him that produced the idea that one in ten people are gay.

Of course, in all of these studies, the data relies on how forthcoming individual participants are about their own sexual history. Whether it's one in eight, nine, or ten, what is important to learn from these studies is that sexual orientation is not a matter of being straight or gay, and it isn't one or the other for a lifetime. We know that young people often experiment when they are young and that many people have come out as gay later in life having never had a homosexual experience. So don't spend too much time trying to lock yourself in a box. Your sexual orientation is unique to you, and it is what it is—perfectly normal.

Coming out is often broken down into phases or stages, and certainly the first and most important phase is coming out to yourself. Almost all of the heterosexual friends I've talked to about this said that they never came out to themselves as straight; they just "went with the flow" like the majority of society does. Some of my male friends described "discovering girls" for the first time, but there wasn't a revelation or notable moment of self-discovery as there often is when you are gay. While I can look back now and clearly identify instances of when I was first attracted to other males, it wasn't until my high school years that I came to the realization that I was gay.

For some people, the point in time when you first realize that you are not straight can be terrifying. But unlike the innate nature of your sexual orientation, the fear and shame you might feel is purely man-made and a product of your social environment. The fear you might feel is produced from what you have learned about from those people who surround your life. It's really important that you understand how fear and shame are different from your sexual orientation because you can fully control fear and shame, but you cannot change your sexual orientation. It is a natural part of your being, whereas fear and shame are not.

I've read stories from people who say it took them years before they "came to terms" with being gay. Denial is a common product of the fear and shame created by one's environment, especially given how oppressive and hateful some parts of our country continue to be toward homosexuality. Denial is a normal reaction to something you don't want or like about yourself. It's a common reaction to many issues, such as being overweight, drinking too much, or other forms of obsessive-compulsive behavior. But these conditions are very different from sexual orientation, as they can be controlled through conscious decision making and positive reinforcement, whereas sexual orientation cannot. Even the American Psychological Association said in August of 2009 that changing one's sexual orientation is not possible. In a report condemning reparative therapy, the APA said that such practices can actually be harmful and lead to suicide.

While it's clear that sexual orientation is not a matter of choice, lifestyle and behavior clearly is. You can be gay but decide to live a straight lifestyle. People have made that choice for centuries. The same is true in the opposite. You can be straight and make a conscious decision to engage in gay sex or even to live a gay lifestyle. But the true nature of your sexual orientation does not change based on the lifestyle you choose to lead.

When I heard straight people say, "I don't understand how you can *choose* to live that lifestyle," I always respond with "Could you *choose* to live a gay lifestyle?" I mean, most of us could probably learn to "fake it" pretty well, but what kind of happiness could you really experience, and why should you have to make that choice? To please someone else? To avoid being criticized or thought less of by someone else? Why do I live a gay lifestyle, you ask? For the same reasons you live a straight lifestyle. Because it is who I am, and I choose to live in the truth for me and no one else.

What sexual behavior you engage in is also a matter of choice and does not have to align with your sexual orientation. Most young people experiment and, as Kinsey found, better than 30 percent of males report having had sex with another man. Does this make them bisexual? Of course not. I've lost count of the number of straight friends I've had in my life who I had sex with on one or more occasion. I suppose if someone said, "I'm straight; I've only experimented with gay sex," I would consider one time truly an experiment. The second time might have been at a different point in time or with a different person. The third time? All I can say is, you like it, and your sexual interest is more than experimentation. And there is nothing at all wrong with that. Some of the straight friends I had sex with are married and have kids. They are very happily married and, as far as I know, do not regularly engage in gay sex. For whatever reason, they made a conscious choice to experiment or decided to have gay sex because they liked it. This experience still does not change the nature of their sexual orientation. Maybe some of them are bisexual and lean to one side or the other of the middle. As Kinsey proved, sexuality is a continuum, not a straight or gay situation.

Discovering and identifying your sexual orientation is the first phase of coming out. The discovery more than likely started when you were very young, but the conscious realization of your sexual orientation most likely didn't happen until your teenage years. Identifying your sexual orientation to yourself is an essential step in your own personal development. Overcoming the fear and shame that you've learned to associate with homosexuality can really get in the way of this self-identification. Denial can prevent it from ever happening.

Becoming conscious of your own sexual orientation and connecting it with an identity requires absolute honesty with yourself. There are all kinds of reasons why people are not able to do this. Feelings of internalized shame and fear can cloud your ability to accept your own truth. But at this stage of coming out, you don't have to worry about anyone accepting who you are other than you. I think it's terrible that the opinions of someone else count for more than one's own opinion of one's self. Another common worry is that of feeling abnormal because of being something other than a heterosexual. The word "normal" means healthy, natural, or regular. While being homosexual or bisexual may not be how the majority of human beings identify, it is nevertheless perfectly normal. As Kinsey discovered, the full range of sexual orientations exist across all races, nationalities, and ethnicities. Others have found it to be equally spread between both genders. The American Psychological Association declared homosexuality to be normal more than thirty years ago, so there is no reason to believe that you are not normal. As a minority, your sexual orientation makes you all that much more special. Resolving your shame and fear of being abnormal is an essential step to moving forward with coming out.

For younger people, it may take time and experience to really discover your sexual orientation. For some people as young as twelve, their sexual orientation emerges clearly and unquestionably. But for many others, it takes some experience to come to a full realization of who they are. Most people are in a good place to make a solid personal assessment by their mid-twenties. However, there is no magic age, no rule, or no time limit for identifying your sexual orientation. And it may change later in your life. Denial, shame, and fear may very well have prevented you from experiencing or exploring the full range and depth of your sexual orientation. It's never too late for self-examination and to acknowledge the truth about this aspect of you.

I can't truly remember a specific day when I looked in the mirror and said, "I'm gay." I think it was more a period of time in my twenties that was often clouded by some hope that I might be bisexual. In my own mind, I thought that somehow having at least a partial attraction to women might somehow make me more acceptable. I did consider if I had an attraction to several women in my life, but it was clear every time that any feelings I had for them were very different from those I had for men. With each time I explored those feelings, I confirmed in my own mind that I was gay, and nothing was going to change about that. It wasn't a matter of meeting the right girl or having the right dating experience. The sexual feelings for women simply were not there and never were.

Bringing your sexual identity to a conscious level can be done in many ways. It can be as simple as recognizing for yourself that you are attracted to the same sex. But confusion, doubt, and uncertainty can sometimes best be worked through by writing in a journal. Writing requires that you consider one thought at a time and that you put down into black-and-white each step of your self-examination. I'm a real fan of writing and particularly of journaling. A journal allows you to go back and revisit thoughts and experiences as you wrote them. You have the opportunity to revisit emotions and feelings that you captured in words as you experienced them. A review can provide you with the ability to look at events and experiences logically and away from the moment in which they occurred.

I never chose to talk with anyone else about what I was feeling and experiencing. I did share sexual experiences with friends who were also experimenting and exploring their own sexual orientation, but we never talked in detail about it. The sexual experiences I shared with friends just happened by either intentional actions on my part or theirs. But talking with confidants, counselors, or therapists can be helpful if you are not able to recognize your sexual orientation on your own. Of course, having these conversations with anyone requires courage and confidence that the matter will remain between the two of you. It requires a high level of trust that you need to consider. Like writing, talking requires you to consider one thought at a time and can make your thinking clearer.

Once you do come to a conclusion, I recommend formalizing your self-recognition in a way that provides you with clarity and personal understanding. Try actually saying out loud, "I'm gay," or "I'm bisexual." Verbalize to yourself your attraction. It may seem silly or be uncomfortable, but saying the words and actually describing your sexual orientation out loud is a powerful step forward toward beginning to live the truth. This action leads to your own ability to fully accept yourself for who you are. You certainly can't expect others to love and accept you if you are unable to accept yourself.

At this point, you should feel some relief or even joy in that you have finally been able to reconcile what may have been causing you confusion for years. You may also experience even more fear about what to do next. The beauty of this phase of coming out is that you are truly in full control of if, when, and who you tell. You may decide to tell no one, and there is certainly no rush to make a big announcement or to throw a coming-out party. The bottom line is that you can move forward from here at your own pace. It is important, though, to now move forward with integrity and total honesty. If you have been dating someone of the opposite sex or claiming to have a boyfriend or girlfriend of the opposite sex to provide a "cover," it is time to stop.

First of all, truly dating someone for the sake of providing a cover is just plain mean and selfish, especially if the other person believes that you are truly connected because of an attraction. If you are lying to those in your life in order to fit in or to avoid suspicions of being gay, stop. I can tell you from experience that the longer you lie, the more difficult and painful it will be to undo the lie with your family and friends. You may fear that you will lose friends if you come out, but I suspect that you will do more harm and chance losing more people in your life from lying than from being who you really are. Lying also furthers the feelings of shame and creates additional fear from being discovered or from "slipping" with the story.

There are many professions in which honesty and being truthful are essential to the ethics of the profession. Law enforcement is one example of a profession in which you may not necessarily be fired for being gay, but you will absolutely be fired for lying. I talk to closeted law enforcement officers all the time about the risk they are putting themselves in by perpetuating a lie about who they are. For a homophobic police chief or sheriff, it would be much easier and accepted as proper and ethical to fire a gay officer for lying than it would for simply being gay. This is also why Don't Ask, Don't Tell policies are particularly dangerous because they force people to lie for the sake of keeping their jobs.

Now that you have accurately identified your sexual orientation, there is a natural desire to further explore that identity and to begin "being" gay. Well, let me say right now that there is no "normal" way of being gay. Society has created and perpetuated certain stereotypes that have no absolute relationship to being gay or what it means to be gay. For example, a stereotype of gay men is that they speak with a lisp, dress in flamboyant clothes, and are overly dramatic. I know there are many others, but now that you are identifying as gay, it doesn't mean that any other aspect of your personality or behavior has to change. You can connect with the community and with gay culture if you chose to without having to become or act within the confines of the stereotypes. Sexual orientation is not represented in how one speaks, walks, or dresses. It is only expressed in who one is attracted to.

The next phase of coming out involves being able to actually establish relationships with other people as you really are. You might consider thinking about identifying circles of people in your life, including your best friends, close friends, family members, extended family, and people at work, both co-workers close to you and those who are simply associates. I found that by first starting with an inner circle of people who are also gay provided me with a foundation and security before I actually started coming out to the straight people in my life. It seems odd, perhaps, to start by telling people you may have never met, but other gay people get it and will have more understanding and support for you, at least at first, than anyone else in your life will likely have to offer. Creating and building a close network of gay friends is an extremely important safety net for your journey out of the closet.

Today, the Internet is an amazing and wonderful source of support and connection with the gay community. You can learn so much about being gay, including everything from how to meet people and dating to health and wellness issues related to being gay. There are some really important things you should learn about here, including the risks of HIV and other sexually transmitted diseases. You may think that you know a lot from your sex education classes in sixth and seventh grade, but there are some unique risks out there while engaging in gay sex that

I'm fairly confident no sex education program covers in even today's most progressive schools.

No matter your age, there are many ways to connect socially with other gay people safely online while maintaining your anonymity. You can speak freely from the safety of your home and talk, perhaps for the first time, very openly about being gay with others. I'm a huge fan of www.gay.com because it has been around a long time, it is a well-operated and reliable website, and it gives you the ability to connect with people by geographic location, age group, or sexual interest. It is not exclusively a site where people are looking for "hook-ups" (meetings exclusively to have sex), whereas many other sites cater for that type of meeting. I guess I might be a little bias because I met my husband on www.gay.com, but I think my own example is a perfect one to make my point. I met Tony after being able to share back and forth our interests and desires. I think that people who are looking for a friendship or something other than a hook-up are more open and play fewer games while chatting online than they do in a bar.

I acknowledge fully that the anonymity of the Internet does provide a perfect place to lie and scam, so use common sense. For example, never give out your personal information online. If you are under eighteen, you shouldn't be socializing online unless your parents know about it, and always be aware that people are not always who they claim to be. Never agree to meet someone for the first time at his or her house, and don't invite strangers over to your house. When I think back to some of the hook-ups I had before and after I came out, I could kick myself for taking some of the huge risks that I did.

Social networking sites like Facebook and MySpace are also great for meeting people, but be very cautious about how you mix your existing friends and family with your outreach to the gay community. I've known several people who were "outed" from information they posted on their social networking site. In fact, there is a trend today with young people coming out by simply posting comments on their social networking page about being gay or queer. For some people this is an effective way of coming out without having to have a face-to-face conversation. I don't recommend giving up that much control at this stage of coming out because of the risk you take by giving up almost all control of this sensitive and important information about you. Focus first on developing connections with other gay people. Look for opportunities to develop friendships with other gay people. And, if a dating situation comes about as a result of this effort, go for it!

Almost every big city has a gay community center or gay social organization of some sort. Many of these organizations host meetings to network, gain support, or just to meet other gay people. There are organizations that support every age group. For example, in my area of California, there are two youth organizations, Positive Images (www. posimages.org) and Spectrum (www.spectrumlgbtcenter.org). There are mens' groups, womens' groups, and an emerging group catering to gay seniors (www.primetimers.org). The best way to find these organizations is to simply search the Internet. Just do a search on "gay (*your city*)." You will be amazed at what comes up, including listings of organizations, gay-friendly businesses, and events occurring in your region.

You may believe that you can create two separate components of your life by having your friends and family in one corner and having your gay friends in the other. You might even think that you can develop an intimate relationship with someone without having your two lives cross paths. Let me assure you that this approach has some significant limitations and will likely result in many short-lived relationships. There will come a point in time when you will want to share all aspects of your life with those you love, and then it will be time to come out to others.

Many of my friends waited to tell others until after they met someone and had a boyfriend or girlfriend, while others, myself included, really wanted to work through coming out to others without the pressure hoping that their families and friends would accept them and who they were dating. There is no proper, polite, or correct way of approaching this next phase, and it will largely be circumstantial. Clearly, if you are not out but you have met someone, you don't have to break up just so you can come out by yourself.

So who do you tell first, and how do you do it? Well, let me start with a few examples of how not to tell someone that you are gay. One of my close friends decided to tell his family at the Thanksgiving dinner table. He figured that he could get it over with all at once and wouldn't have to worry about his mother getting hysterical in front of all of his aunts, uncles, and cousins. It went something like this: "Mom, I gay.

Pass the mashed potatoes, please." Talk about a situation that is totally out of control and filled with unknown risk. I heard this story shortly after I first came out and have to admit that I loved it. In fact, "passing the mashed potatoes" became the code among my gay friends every time I came out to someone new. But the Thanksgiving dinner table is not the time or place.

One mistake I made with a close friend was to make it a guessing game at a party with a lot of other people around who didn't know and with no place to talk with my friend privately. My game playing actually came across as an attempt to trick my friend into going to a party that he otherwise would not have attended simply because he wanted to know what I was trying to get him to guess about. Having a private place to talk is important, especially if there is a history between the two of you that you need to "undo" or explain. Remember, in every case with every person you tell, you've likely known that you are gay for a long time, but it may be the first time the person you are telling has even considered this about you. Even your friends need time to "come out" and to think and talk through what you are sharing with them.

Another terrible mistake to make is to start out by saying to a friend, "I have a very personal secret to tell you, and you have to promise not to tell anyone else." I suppose there is nothing wrong with asking your friend for his or her confidence, but don't expect for one minute that he or she will be able to hold that secret. What I mean to say is that you really need to be prepared for the world to know that you are gay because you cannot absolutely control the actions of anyone else no matter how close of a friend he or she is. So until you are ready to move to the next phase of coming out, don't tell anyone.

In my case, I dated a lot over the years but never actually told any of my straight friends or family. I did what I said not to do, which was to create a fictitious cover story riddled with lies. I finally came to a point in my life where I was tired of lying and really tired of feeling unfulfilled. But I didn't know where to start, so I looked for friend who I discovered was also gay. This person was a new friend in my life and one with whom I also had only a professional relationship. This added an additional layer of risk because I could have created problems for myself at work had he not accepted my news well. But I knew he was the right person to tell, and that is my best advice to you. Think about your friends and people in your family, and don't rush to the first person who calls you after you identify as being gay.

Once you get a foundation of gay friends surrounding you, start thinking about the next circle of people in your life who you want to tell. Hopefully, this circle includes your very best friends and people who you know will be accepting of you. It's always ideal to experience success with the first few people you tell, but don't let a disappointment or rejection stop you from living your life in the truth. Your purpose for telling someone in your life that you are gay is not to get his or her approval. The purpose is to share an important part of you that will enable your friend to know all of the real you. It's always possible that you will overestimate how someone will hear your news, but you must cast aside the requirement that the other person accept you. And it's also important that you not take on a feeling of shame because of how someone else reacts to you. The power of how you feel must remain in your control and in your hands, so if you are not yet capable of maintaining that kind of control, you are not ready to share your news. It's taken you this long to accept yourself, and you don't need to risk growing the shame you feel based on how a best friend reacts. But if you are feeling confident and proud, share who you are and enjoy the wonderful and liberating feeling that comes with ridding yourself of this secret.

For most people, parents will be the most challenging people to talk with, and no matter your age, there is no reason you have to start with them. As a young person, I do encourage you to talk with your parents, but they do not have to be the first people you tell. Unfortunately, I also have friends who confided in their parents only to be cast out onto the streets. They literally became homeless. As horrific as it is to imagine how parents could so quickly dismiss the children they created, it happens at an alarming rate. If you are under eighteen and living at home, use your own judgment about telling your parents. You will know better than anyone how accepting or not they will be. You can still reach out to gay youth organizations for support without your parents knowing or having to give you permission.

For whatever reason, a lot of people care very deeply about what their parents think, and being accepted by their parents is of monumental importance even later in life. Having my parents accept me was extremely important, and it caused me great fear as I thought about how to tell them that I was gay. But here is another angle to consider. Most parents look forward to watching their children grow up, fall in love, create a family, and sharing all of those moments and milestones with their children. Parents yearn to see their children happy, and they find satisfaction in seeing this happen. When you deny who you are, you deny your parents the chance to see you happy, to enjoy time with you and your boyfriend, girlfriend, partners, husband, or wife. In today's world, a gay couple can have children if they wish, and the hopes and dreams of your parents can be realized together with you. I realize that not all parents will want or accept you in a "gay family," but if you keep this part of your life a secret from them, you are denying your parents the opportunity to accept you and to be part of your own personal joy.

In my case, I told my sister in person, and—fortunately for me—she doesn't keep secrets well. She told my mom and my aunt, and all were much more accepting and loving than I could have ever hoped for. In my dad's case, I chose to send him a letter. A letter can give the reader a chance to think about your disclosure alone without the pressure of having to respond "appropriately." It also relieves you of the pressure of having to look that person in the face and say, "I'm gay." There are even greeting cards designed for this purpose. Don't think for a minute that a letter is impersonal or cold. In fact, sending a letter to someone you care about and taking the time to share your news in a very personal way, to me, is a very loving gesture. I used this method with only one other person in my life, and it was someone who I wanted to know but didn't wish to have further communication with.

As you move forward in your life, coming out to someone won't require going out for a special lunch or a carefully worded letter. You will do it without really thinking about it by introducing your significant other or by talking on Monday with co-workers about what you did on your weekend and who you did it with. Perhaps you will come out by having pictures of you and your partner on your desk. But don't assume a bunch of pictures will take care of this disclosure for you. Some people just don't get it. I have several pictures of Tony and me in my office. One of my newer employees came to see me and in the course of our conversation asked, "Hey, who is the dude in the picture with you?" I said, "Oh, that is my partner, Tony." This employee knew that I worked in law enforcement and apparently assumed that Tony was my work partner, because later that day, he offered some fruit from his yard to take home to my *wife*. Of course, you aren't obligated to come out to everyone you meet, so after telling the people who really matter to you in your life, I suggest just living your life and let people learn about you through the normal course of conversation.

## If I Had Only Known Then What I Know Now

I am frequently asked what I would have done differently if given he chance to give myself advice before coming out. Coincidentally, while finishing this book, I was asked to write for a feature article published on Gay.com a letter to myself with advice about coming out. The letter was to be dated before coming out and to contain advice based on what I learned after coming out. Here is the full, unedited version of that letter.

> October 11, 2003
> Dear Greg,
> Last spring, I remember how much you were dreading the fact that you were turning forty. You complained about getting old and, to yourself, about being lonely and unclear about what the future might hold. To your credit, you made turning forty a celebration of life rather than a period of mourning and, while you discovered that the day you actually did turn forty didn't feel much different from your last day being thirty nine, let me assure you that in March of next year, you are truly going to feel young and reborn. On March 4, 2004, you are going to become the true and full person you were born to be and in the years that follow, you will discover the happiness you have been searching for the last 25 years.
>
> Next February, you will meet a student in your class who you will soon discover is probably gay. Although you will not know with absolute certainty, there will be

plenty of clues. He will defy your stereotypes and you will see, for the first time, pieces of yourself in him. Reasoning and caution will tell you to say away, but your heart and your gut will tell you that he is the one you will share your most intimate secret with. Have confidence in what you have read in books about the idea that people come into your life at certain times for a specific purpose. There is a reason he is in your class this coming spring. The last minute change in assignment for you to be his teacher at this point in your life is no mistake and this is all you need to know. Go with your gut and your heart, he is the one to tell.

Now I know after spending 25 years working hard at hiding the fact that you are gay from so many people, even at times from yourself, cannot be undone in one night. But just like the fall of the Berlin Wall, it must start and on March 10, 2004, the wall you have built around you, the wall that has protected you from hate and from the fear of rejection will crumble as you say three words out loud to your student, "I am gay." Yes, your heart will be pounding and the risks you will be taking are very real, but trust me, it will be so worth it. You will meet for dinner at Applebee's. He will share his coming out story with you first and then it will be your turn.

It is hard for me to put into words the feelings of pure joy, relief, and freedom you will experience almost immediately following your disclosure. Your body will tingle with excitement and a sense of liberty, youthfulness, and wholeness like you have never felt before. Oh yes, you will have your share of doubt about what you just did, but it will be done and there will be no going back. Suddenly you will feel an enormous shift in your life. As you look back, you will wonder why you waited so long to say those words out loud.

Now you can forget all of the fake names and alibis you used for those chance meetings and one night stands. In fact, in nine months from now, you will meet Tony, the man you will spend the rest of your life with. You will even marry him.

For now, here is some advice to get you through the next few months. Coming out is a journey, not a destination. You will be coming out for the rest of your life, but know it gets easier all the time. Take your time telling people your truth. Build yourself a strong network of gay friends and learn about this part of your history. Go visit the Castro in San Francisco, experience the "gay scene," and get to know yourself all over again. You do not need to change anything about yourself other than to make a commitment to never lie about who you really are again. It will not be easy at first and it might be uneasy for many years every time you have to disclose you are gay, but rest assured, you are not alone and know that people will be as comfortable around and with you as you are with yourself. Do not spend a single moment feeling like you have to make up for lost time or that, somehow, you have wasted years of your life hiding. You will feel some regret about waiting so long, but get over it because you cannot go back in time no matter how hard you try.

As for other people in your life, do not under estimate the love they have for you. Give your friends and family some credit. I mean, come on, you are forty, have never been married; you have a good job and they have never seen you date a woman. They probably already know or at least suspect. I know you like parties, but do not throw a coming out party and make a big announcement to everyone all at once. Instead, make a list, sit down with your closest friends, and let them know one at a time. They are not going to run from you or reject you. In fact, your true friends will embrace your truth and will want to know more. Oh, be prepared for your friend Mark, one of the first people you tell, to ask you about what type of guys you are attracted too. He is also going to end up wanting to celebrate his thirtieth birthday with you and his wife in the Castro. Do not worry about when he is dancing with you at the Café; it's only the third time in his entire life that he has danced with anyone. He is not gay; he just loves and supports you.

Your parents are not going to reject your either. I know you fear telling your dad the most, but he will love you even more after you tell him than he does now. Take your time, but do not deny you parents from being able to share who you love any more. All they care about is that you are happy. Be patient, listen to them, and do not be afraid to talk to them.

As for work, the cops will probably talk behind your back and the homophobes will go crazy with your news, but the rumors about you have been out there for years. People will talk less now that the truth is out, because the truth really isn't much to talk or rumor about. You will not get fired and, in fact, you career will blossom with even more opportunities for doing what you love, teaching and trying to make law enforcement a better profession. A few closeted gay students in your future classes will make themselves visible to you because you will be an example of who they can become. You will demonstrate that they too can come out and still be successful in law enforcement. They will tell you that you have been the role model for what is possible and that you have given them hope. Crazy, isn't it?

I'm glad you are not waiting until National Coming Out Day next October to come out. You do not need a special day to come out, just a little bit of encouragement and the right person to tell. I say go for it and share your truth with the world.

All the best,

Greg

## Reconciling Your Religion

If you are not religious or identify as being spiritual, you may feel a void of one kind or another, but you may have avoided a personal struggle that many people cannot overcome. I can't express how fortunate I am to have been raised in the Catholic Church and to have never struggled with my faith for a second. I've talked to so many other people who are Catholic, Mormon or some other form of Christianity who just cannot get past the fear and guilt imposed upon them by spiritual leaders and their faith. How I got so lucky, I'm not entirely sure, but I have read a lot about religion and sexual orientation and will share my interpretations of that research.

I think one of the ideas that made it easier for me is that I recognized early on that churches are man-made organizations operated by human beings. The Bible is collection of stories written by humans thousands of years ago. I acknowledge that faith means believing in things that you can't necessarily see or prove, but how church leaders interpret and communicate the meaning of the Bible varies tremendously and always has. It's all about who you decide to believe. Gay people are not the only victims of biblical criticism. Women and racial minorities have been targets of religious zealots in the past. Religious and political leaders have used the power of society's faith in the Bible to promote their own ideas and to rationalize voting rights and slavery. In today's world, gay people are being targeted with this very powerful weapon, and it's causing incredible harm.

If you are deeply religious, chances are that your faith is deeply rooted, and reconciling your faith with your sexual orientation is critically important to eliminating shame and being able to live an authentic life. It's really worth the time to read some of the modern writing on this topic, and I will share with you some of the books and authors I recommend that you pay attention to. These are credible sources that are as much or more experienced in theology as any of the loud-mouthed religious zealots who are ready to condemn gay people to hell.

Bishop Gene Robinson, the first openly gay man to be installed as an Episcopal bishop, wrote a book and participated in a documentary, both of which I highly recommend. *For the Bible Tells Me So* is a documentary that explores how the Bible has been interpreted over the centuries and how it is misinterpreted today. In his book *In the Eye of the Storm*, Bishop Robinson explains that the Bible was written using language and context in the time it was written. We rely on trained and ordained ministers of a church to interpret the meaning of those words for us. The Old Testament has references to homosexuality, the most infamous of which is found in Leviticus. However, the New Testament has no direct reference to homosexuality. Christian churches preach accepting Jesus Christ as your savior, and that's all well and good for gay people because Christ never talked about homosexuality (at least that was recorded in the Bible).

The hypocrisy in how Leviticus is interpreted, preached, and applied is perhaps the most egregious example of how conservative and unethical Christian preachers use the Bible to attack gay people. In the same way that Leviticus suggests that for men to lay with other men is an abomination, in the same chapter, it is also an abomination to eat shrimp. Leviticus also prohibits cutting your hair or beard. Those who preach strict adherence to the Bible selectively apply a literal meaning only to the sections they chose. You can't have it both ways and keep it believable.

There is nothing wrong with religious faith and a belief in God, Buddha, Allah, or any other higher power. All forms of religion require faith and belief in something that isn't seen or that can be absolutely proven. Believe in your faith and hold onto your religion for all of the good things it can do for enriching and guiding your life. Be careful about the other human beings you decide to believe in and whose interpretation of the Bible you decided to accept. Remember that these individuals come from the same time period you do, and no one on this earth was present the day the Bible, the Koran, or the Torah were written. Think about some of the fundamentals of your faith that are in the Bible, and I'm sure you have heard your minister say, "God created man in his own image." If you believe this, then you must also believe that God created you and your sexual orientation.

## About the Law

The laws in our states as related to sexual orientation are literally all over the map in what they say about hate crimes, adoption, marriage, and employment law. About the only thing that has been universally reconciled across the country is the law related to sodomy and hate crimes. In fact, most sexual contact between two consenting adults, regardless of their gender, is now legal. But it wasn't that long ago that most forms of sexual contact between two consenting adults of the same gender would land you time in prison. Federal hate crimes law was changed in October of 2009 with the Matthew Shepard and James Byrd, Jr. Hate Crimes Prevention Act. Federal law was changed to include sexual orientation, gender identity, and disability to the list of identities protected. The law was also expanded to include any crime of physical violence motivated by the victim's actual or perceived race, nationality, religion, sexual orientation, gender identity, and disability. It took twelve years to get this law changed from when it was first introduced by the late Senator Edward Kennedy.

The United States Supreme Court has not been friendly to gay rights issues throughout its history and, in my opinion, has been reluctantly responsive to the suits brought before them by gay victims of all kinds of discrimination. In contrast, we have a federal constitution and the Bill of Rights that guarantees general freedoms that obviously apply to nonheterosexual people. The Fourteenth Amendment is very clear in its guarantee of equal rights for all people. And yet, state supreme courts and the US Supreme Court have been very slow to right many wrongs that seem so clearly to be in violation of these ideals. The right of same-sex couples to marry is today's gay rights issue and one that I'm sure, based on its history, the US Supreme Court will be reluctant to consider, but a case may rise to this level sooner than you think.

In 2010, two suits were filed in federal court—one in Massachusetts and one in California—both dealing with same-sex marriage. The Massachusetts case involved a legally married same-sex couple who sued the federal government because they could not access federal rights associated with marriage because of the Defense of Marriage Act (DOMA) signed into law by President George W. Bush. The federal district court ruled that DOMA violated the Tenth Amendment of the United States Constitution because Congress overextended its authority by enacting a law that violated the sovereignty of the states. The second case was filed in California and involved same-sex couples who were denied the right to marry based on the now infamous Proposition 8. California law allows an initiative to be put on the ballot and approved by a simple majority. Proposition 8 changed the California State Constitution to include a definition of recognized marriage to being one only between a man and a woman. This case alleges that Proposition 8 violates the Fourteenth Amendment to the United States Constitution. It's sure that both of these cases will end up being appealed all the way up to the United States Supreme Court within the next ten years.

Be that as it may, it is important to understand where we stand today regarding the law and all of its facets. One of the concerns most people have when they come out is about any threat there now may be to their employment status. According to the Human Rights Campaign (www.hrc.org), only twenty-one states and the District of Columbia prohibit employment discrimination based on sexual orientation. That means that you can fire someone from his or her job, deny a promotion or special assignment, or refuse to hire someone at all because of the person's sexual orientation in over half of the states in this country. There is no federal protection for employment discrimination like there is for race and gender. There is, however, pending legislation known as the Employment Non-Discrimination Act (ENDA) that will add sexual orientation to the list of reasons for which no employer in any state may discriminate.

At this point in time, there is risk, and you should evaluate your own individual situation before you come out at work. The Human Rights Campaign has a section of their website devoted to outlining the laws in each state that apply to being gay, including interstate relationship recognition, hospital visitation, housing, parenting, employment, marriage, relationship recognition, hate crimes, and school laws and policies. It's worth getting to know what laws and protections, if any, exist in your state.

## Be Involved in Creating Change

If you have been closeted for an extended period in your life, you may not have felt a stake in the fight for gay rights. I mentioned earlier in this book that as a white male who was deeply closeted, I benefited from a position of privilege throughout my life. The civil rights movement was something I watched take place as a spectator. I never felt a direct connection to the gay rights aspect of this movement because it didn't directly touch my life. Now having been out for six years, I have an emotional and personal connection to the movement, and my guess is that most people who come out later in life will experience that connection as I did.

Everyone in our community needs to be involved at some level in the fight for equality and civil rights. You may not want to get married, adopt children, or get a job in state without employment protection, but the rights we are fighting for are those protecting the choice—your choice as an American citizen. It's like so many of the other rights we have that you may or may not decide to exercise. Freedom of speech, religion, and assembly are all rights that protect your choice to engage or not. Why should you be denied a right of choice because of your sexuality? I'm not talking about additional or special rights not currently offered to heterosexual people; I'm talking about basic civil rights to make choices already available to the majority of American citizens.

There are many people who have worked very hard to make the gains we've realized today. These pioneers have suffered physically, mentally, and emotionally, and I feel that we owe it to their legacies to continue the pursuit of equality. With all of this said, you don't have to become an independent activist out there on your own to make a meaningful contribution to the fight for civil rights. There are many reputable organizations operating at the national, state, and local level that would love your help and support. The Human Rights Campaign (HRC) is the largest national organization advocating for gay rights in the country. The National Center for Lesbian Rights (www.nclrights. org) is working hard on employment-related laws impacting both gay males and females. If you want to focus your efforts on youth, the Gay, Lesbian, and Straight Education Network (www.glsen.org) is one of the premier gay youth organizations that fight for anti-bullying laws and that support the gay-straight alliances in our schools. Stop the

Hate (www.stophate.org) is an educational initiative of Campus Pride (www.campuspride.org) and provides training programs for colleges and universities on how to prevent bias and hate crimes. Maybe you are like me and have a person or organization that touched your life that is working for gay rights. The Matthew Shepard Foundation (www.matthewshepard.org) is working to prevent hate violence directed at the gay community by providing a variety of educational programs that support gay youth.

You will find all kinds of organizations working at the state level like Equality California (www.eqca.org). There are, of course, many local organizations supporting everything from gay youth to HIV/AIDS care. Whatever the cause that strikes your interest, get involved at some level. It can be as easy as giving money and as involved as participating on a board of directors. Every one of these groups is some sort of nonprofit organization and is required to operate with a board of directors. Local groups sometimes struggle to find talented and dedicated people to serve on their boards.

There are other ways to advance our cause, as well, including attending fundraising and education programs sponsored by gay rights groups, blogging, writing letters to the editor, and voting for candidates who represent our interests and who support equality for the gay community. Voting for the right candidate is something you can do immediately, today, without having to come out and without having to expose yourself if you are not ready to become visible. People underestimate the power of the voting process for creating change. I can tell you that the right legislator can make all the difference in the world. Your voice counts, so make sure your candidate represents your interests.

## Welcome to the Community

The gay experience is unique, and there is a really wonderful community waiting for you to come out and to be part of it. The gay community transcends race, nationality, ethnicity, age, and gender. It is a common attribute shared throughout the human race. We have a culture with a history and many exciting traditions. Without a doubt, you learned none of this in school. Spend some time learning about your culture and your community. You can do this, too, from the privacy of your own computer simply by searching "gay history."

For law enforcement personnel, there is an emerging network of gay officer action leagues, law enforcement gay action leagues, and gay peace officer associations with hundreds of members in states all over the country who are also ready and waiting to embrace you. I talked about the importance of establishing a network of gay friends as part of your foundation while working your way through the coming-out process. As a law enforcement officer, it's really important to connect with other gay law enforcement professionals. The law enforcement profession has some unique challenges, not the least of which is widespread homophobia. Your peers and colleagues in the profession are really in the best place to give you advice. Listen to their stories, and learn from their mistakes. Most importantly, be authentic, be yourself, and live your life well.

# RESOURCES

You are not alone. There are literally thousands of "out" gay, lesbian, bisexual, and transgender people who are working successfully in law enforcement, the fire service, or as emergency medical services professionals. While this book has offered you just a few examples of what is possible when you come out, there are many lesbian, gay, bisexual, and transgender police officers, firefighters, and EMS professionals out there for you connect with and talk to through some of the LGBT professional organizations that exist throughout the United States. You can always find an updated list of these organizations with links to their respective websites on our website at www.comingoutfrombehindthebadge.com.

There is a national networking website that offers a place for any member or prospective member of law enforcement to connect with others at www.bluepride.org. Associated with this website is a biweekly radio program broadcast on the Internet called *Blue Pride Radio* at www.blueprideradio.com. You can listen online from anywhere in the world, and, again, you will find links to this radio show on our website. There are two common titles for the LGBT law enforcement organizations, including LEGAL (Law Enforcement Gay Action League) and GOAL

(Gay Officers Action League). Both of these organizations are affiliated with LEGAL International. Collectively, these organizations present an annual conference that is held in a different location around the United States. In 2011, the fifteenth annual conference will be held in Las Vegas, Nevada. I cannot say enough about the value of attending these conferences. In addition to being able to attend some amazing training presentations, attendees have the ability to network with other LGBT professionals in an environment like no other. It is both empowering and nurturing.

The international organization, located here in the United States, supports transgender law enforcement professionals. TCOPS (Transgender Community of Police and Sheriffs) has a website with information and support at www.tcops-international.org/LEwebsites.html.

For the fire service and emergency medical services professionals, there is the National EMS and Firefighters Pride Alliance at www.mynefpa.org. This organization offers pages of a variety of social networking websites like Facebook that are specifically for firefighters and for EMS professionals.

Here is a list of the LGBT public safety professional organizations that we knew about at the time this book was printed.

## Association Websites

National EMS and Firefighters Pride Alliance (National)
www.mynefpa.org

Fire Flag/EMS
www.fireflag.org

Gay Officers Action League of Chicago—GOAL
www.goal-chicago.org

Gay Officers Action League of Iowa—GOAL
E-mail:goal.iowa@gmail.com

Gay Officers Action League of Michigan—GOAL
E-mail: goalmi@aol.com

Gay Officers Action League of New York—GOAL
www.goalny.org

Gay Officers Action League of New England—GOAL
www.goalne.org

Law Enforcement Gays and Lesbians of Alabama—LEGAL
www.alabamalegal.org

Law Enforcement Gays and Lesbians of Florida—LEGAL
www.fla-legal.com

Lesbian Gay Peace Officers Association of Austin, Texas—LGPOA
www.lgpoa-austin.org

Protect and Defend
www.protectanddefend.org

Serving With Pride—Canada
www.servingwithpride.ca

Transgender Community of Police and Sheriffs (TCOPS)
www.tcops-international.org/LEwebsites.html


## LGBT Law Enforcement Professional Organizations by Region

### Western United States

GSPOA—Northern California Golden State Peace Officers
Association
PO Box 14006
San Francisco, CA 94114-0006
Phone: 415-281-0610
E-mail: gspoanorca@aol.com

GSPOA—Southern California Golden State Peace Officers Association
of Southern California
1125 N. McCadden Place
Los Angeles, CA 90038
Phone: 323-962-5555
E-mail: gspoa@gspoa.com

GOAL—Washington State Northwest GOAL
c/o Officer Linda Lane
810 Third Street, Suite 140–45
Seattle, WA 98104
Phone: 206-684-5729
E-mail: nw-goal@halcyon.com

Vision—Oregon Vision
1352 NE Forty-Seventh Ave.
Portland, OR 97213
Phone: 503-284-4083
E-mail: pdxcop911@aol.com

COPSA—Colorado Public Safety Alliance
4557 N. Bearlily Way
Castle Rock, Colorado 80104
Phone: 303-663-6617
E-mail: coloradopsa@aol.com

AAPSP—Arizona Association of Public Safety Professionals
PO Box 207
Tempe, Arizona 85280-0207
Phone: 602-534-6219
E-mail: aapsp@aol.com

## Northeastern United States

GOAL—DC GOAL—DC Gay Officers Action League—District of
Columbia
E-mail: goaldc@hotmail.com

GOAL NY Region One Gay Officers Action League
New York City Region One Post Office
PO Box 2038 Canal Street Station
New York, NY 10013
Phone: 1-212-NY1-GOAL or 1-212-691-4625
E-mail: ny1goal@goalny.org

GOAL—New York State GOAL NYS
PO Box 2038 Canal Street Station
New York, NY 10013
Phone: 1-888-NYS-GOAL or 1-888-697-4625 or 518-462-6138 Ext 61
E-mail: goalnys@aol.com

GOAL—New Jersey Gay Officers Action League New Jersey Division
PO Box 10133
Brunswick, NJ 08906
Phone: 1-888-GOAL-NJ2 or 201-489-0895
E-mail: njgoal@aol.com

GOAL—New England Gay Officers Action League New
England—Boston
PO Box 587
Boston, MA 02117
Phone: 617-376-3612
E-mail: info@goalne.org

MDGLEA—Maryland MDGLEA—Maryland Gay Law Enforcement
Association
E-mail: Marylandglea@aol.com


## Southern United States

Texas LGPOA—Austin Post Office
PO Box 19817
Austin, Texas 78760-9817
Contact: Steven McCormick, President
E-mail: lgpoaaustin@gmail.com
Facebook: LGPOA—Austin

Florida LEGAL, Inc.—Florida
c/o Key West Police Department
525 Angela Street
Key West, FL 33040
Phone: 305-292-8200
E-mail: flalegal@fla-legal.com
Contact: Sgt. Alan Newby, President—Florida LEGAL

GOAL/GA—Atlanta, GA GOAL / GA
Contact: Tony Leonard
Phone: 404-688-9920
E-mail: goalatlanta@aol.com
Website: www.ga-legal.org

Alabama LEGAL LGBT LEO Support Organization
Website: www.alabamalegal.org

## Midwestern United States

GOAL—Illinois Gay Officers Action League—Illinois
PO Box 578750
Chicago, IL 60657-8750
Phone: 312-409-4127
E-mail: goalil95@aol.com
Website: www.goal-chicago.org

Lesbian and Gay Police Association—Illinois Lesbian and Gay Police
Association
PO Box 388621
Chicago, IL 60638
Phone: 312-409-4881
E-mail: suekar@suba.com

LEGAL of Minnesota—SD MN ND IA WI LEGAL of Minnesota
E-mail: legalmn@aol.com
Ohio Lesbian Gay Police Association
1594 Bryden Road
Columbus, OH 43205
Phone: 614-253-3144
E-mail: ltmike@ameritech

LEGAL—Canada Law Enforcement Gay Alliance (LEGAL)
PO Box 234 Station P
Toronto, ON M5S 2S7 CANADA
Phone: 416-339-0210

LEGAL—British Columbia Law Enforcement Gays and Lesbians of British Columbia
103-13630 Seventy-Second Avenue
Surrey BC V3W 2P3 CANADA
E-mail: legalbc@axionet.com

The Ottawa Police Gay and Lesbian Liaison Committee UK Gay Police Association
Serving with Pride
Canada PO Box 46041
777 Bay Street
Toronto, ON M5G 2P6 canada
Website: www.gay.police.uk
Website: www.servingwithpride.ca

AUSTRALIA GALPEN-VIC—(Gay and Lesbian Employees Network of Victoria)
Websites: http://groups.msn.com/galpenvic
http://groups.msn.com/galpenvic/_whatsnew.msnw

# BIBLIOGRAPHY

Downs, Alan. *The Velvet Rage*. Cambridge, Massachusetts: Da Capo Press, 2005.

Robinson, Gene. *In the Eye of the Storm*. New York, New York: Seabury Books, 2008.

*In re Marriage Cases*, 43 Cal.4th 757, 183 P.3d 384, 76 Cal.Rptr.3d 683, May 15, 2008.

*Data From Alfred Kinsey's Studies*. Retrieved June 1, 2010, from The Kinsey Institute For Research: http://www.kinseyinstitute.org/research/ak-data.html, 1996.

Edwards Brothers Malloy
Oxnard, CA  USA
October 22, 2015